Mission Possible
One-Year Devotional for Young Readers

Mission Possible
One-Year Devotional
for Young Readers

✝✝✝

365 Days of Encouragement
for Living a Life That Counts

Tim Tebow

with A. J. Gregory

WaterBrook

Introduction

Do you wonder if God really has a plan for your life? Do you ask yourself questions like these?

- *What difference can I make?*
- *Does anything I do really matter?*

Maybe what I'm talking about is all new to you. Maybe you've never thought about your life beyond school and friends and video games. If that's the case, I'm about to rock your world. I want to introduce you to the idea of purpose.

Purpose is a big deal, but it's also a lot simpler than you may think. Ultimately, as followers of Jesus Christ, our purpose is to know God and make Him known. And we do that by loving and serving Him and others.

You are holding this book in your hand right now because you want to make your life count. You want to make a difference, but you're not exactly sure where to start and how to keep going. Well, guess what? God wants to use *you* within His great plan for humanity. He has a plan and a purpose for *your* life! And I'm going to be with you for the next 365 days to help you discover what that is.

This devotional is broken down into a wide range of topics that are going to teach you what it takes to live a mission-possible life, including the basics of a mission mindset, what it really means to sacrifice, and how weakness can actually be a strength. You'll also have a chance to hear from some special people in my life, people we've served through the Tim Tebow Foundation (TTF) who have graciously offered to share words of comfort, hope, and challenge through their perspective of what it means to live mission possible.

In addition to multiple themed devotionals, twice a month you'll read through a prayer I've written for you using a combination of different passages in Scripture. To get the most out of the prayer, look up these verses in the translation of your choice and spend time meditating on them.

What I call mission essentials also appear approximately quarterly. These devotionals target timeless truths to keep you encouraged, anchored, and focused on God as you continue to live mission possible.

Be sure to keep a prayer journal or notebook handy so you can jot down answers to the questions at the end of each devotional. Or feel free to write in the margins, if you prefer.

Take your time reading these devos. Don't rush through them. Give yourself a chance to hear God speak to your heart and offer you some spiritual training.

Let's start making each day count, together.

Mission Possible
One-Year Devotional for Young Readers

A Prayer for Newness

✝

Dear God,

Thank You for being the Maker of all things new. As someone who trusts in Jesus, I believe that what You say in the Bible is true. The old has gone and the new is here. I am a new creation. Today is a new day.

Help me to make good decisions and say goodbye to bad habits and bad attitudes. Remind me that I am Your child, and help me to grow in You.

When I get overwhelmed, remind me that I am Your masterpiece—that even before I was born, You created me to do good works in Your name. I pray those things come to pass in their right time.

As I begin to read and grow through these devotions, teach me to value what's most important. Thank You for leading and guiding me.

In Jesus's name I pray. Amen.

Based on: 2 Corinthians 5:17; Isaiah 43:18–19; Romans 12:2; Ephesians 2:10; 1:18

The Greatest Trade

✝

If anyone is in Christ, this person is a new creation;
the old things passed away; behold, new things have come.
2 Corinthians 5:17

In 1975, in what was probably one of the worst trades in sports history, the Milwaukee Bucks traded Kareem Abdul-Jabbar to the Los Angeles Lakers. Abdul-Jabbar would go on to win five championship titles and a record *six* MVPs. There have been plenty of other disappointing trades in the athletic world, which makes me grateful for being on the receiving end of the greatest trade in history.

When God gives us the chance to change our sin for the righteousness of Christ, He offers us the opportunity to go from old to new. From dead to alive. Darkness to light. Bondage to freedom. Separation from God to united with Christ. Lost to found. We don't have to earn or work for salvation. Jesus paid the price for us.

When we accept Jesus, we are made right with God, and we experience the joy of a new, purpose-filled life. So live out of that joy. You have been traded to the greatest team of all: the family of God!

How does being reminded that you are part of the greatest trade of all make you feel?

You Are a Divine Work of Art

+

We are His workmanship, created in Christ Jesus
for good works, which God prepared beforehand
so that we would walk in them.
Ephesians 2:10

Many people spend their lives hoping to fit in. Maybe you've worn the same brands or listened to the same music as everyone else, more to feel like you belong than because you really like those things. It's funny how hard we can attempt to be something we're not.

Trying to fit in is a solid strategy for living an average life. But God didn't call you to be average. He didn't make you the same as everyone else. When the apostle Paul called us God's workmanship, he used the Greek word *poiema*, which means "the works of God as creator."[1] Some translations use "masterpiece" instead of "workmanship."

When you begin to see yourself as God sees you, trying to fit in is going to be a lot less important to you. Be free to be who God says you are. You matter too much to Him to be just like everyone else.

**How does knowing you are a masterpiece created
for good works make you feel about yourself?**

God Is Looking for You

✛

The eyes of the LORD roam throughout the earth, so that
He may strongly support those whose heart is completely His.
2 Chronicles 16:9

God wants to help you live a mission-possible life. This can be
done only through Him.

The verse above talks about how God is looking for people
who are loyal to Him. The words were spoken by a prophet called
Hanani to King Asa of Judah, the southern kingdom of Israel. King
Asa had once relied on God to deliver him from a fierce enemy.
God had come through and proved His faithfulness. For the next
thirty-five years, King Asa enjoyed a peaceful reign. However, when
Baasha, the king of the northern kingdom of Israel, threatened to
invade Judah, King Asa's dependence on God shattered. Instead of
seeking help from God, King Asa looked elsewhere. Hanani scolded
the king and reminded him that God looks for people who wholeheartedly seek Him.

It seems much easier at times to depend on ourselves or others
rather than on a God we cannot see. Yet He is looking for the heart
that is committed to Him. Will His eyes land on you?

**What is holding you back from
being all in with God?**

Aim for Significance

✝

What good will it do a person if he gains
the whole world, but forfeits his soul?
Matthew 16:26

I believe that one of the greatest tragedies is to reach the end of one's life and look back and say, "I was successful in things that did not matter." I want you to be successful, but more than anything, I want you to be *significant*. When you live for Jesus and you love people, you're going to have a life of significance.

I think of success as being focused on self, reaching certain dreams, or excelling in whatever goals we have assigned ourselves. But significance has an outward reach. When we succeed, we influence our own lives; when we are significant, we influence the lives of others. To achieve lasting significance, you have to find a need and use your gifts to meet it. Begin by serving others with the gifts God has given you. Use whatever you have—a lot or a little—for the good of others. To be truly successful, aim for significance.

What's one way significance is greater than success?

Willingness Is What Is Required

✛

If you are willing and obedient,
You will eat the best of the land.
Isaiah 1:19

A mission-possible life is not about ability; it's about being will-ing. When Moses was *eighty years old,* he was working as a shepherd for his father-in-law. We're not sure what his future plans were at that point, but everything changed when God spoke to him through a burning bush. God told Moses to return to Egypt, the place from which he had fled forty years earlier, and lead the nation of Israel out of captivity. But Moses hardly seemed the man for the job. He told God this, listing five reasons why God must have got-ten His wires crossed:

1. "I don't have the ability" (see Exodus 3:11).
2. "I don't know enough" (see verse 13).
3. "What if the people don't believe me?" (see 4:1).
4. "But I'm the worst speaker ever!" (see verse 10).
5. "Send someone else" (see verse 13).

But God didn't let his excuses keep the mission from moving forward. He was waiting for Moses to offer his willingness. Eventu-ally, Moses carried out an incredible rescue mission.

A mission-possible life is not about being ready; it's about being willing.

What's your excuse for not living mission possible?

Choose to Discover

✛

Taste and see that the LORD is good;
How blessed is the man who takes refuge in Him!
Psalm 34:8

I believe that the greatest form of love is to act in the best interests of another person. That's exactly what Jesus did for you and me and the rest of humankind. He loves us without limits, without reserve, without measure.

God wants to have a relationship with you. Not just one where you show up at church once a week or say the same prayer each time you wolf down a meal. He wants you to know Him. He wants you to talk to Him. The ancient king David, who experienced his share of highs and lows, wrote a beautiful psalm persuading us to "taste and see that the LORD is good." Don't just take his word for it (or mine). Commit to pursuing God for the next year through meditating on these devotions. Discover for yourself what it's like to know the God of the universe's unconditional love.

**What is one step you can do, starting today,
to get to know God better?**

His Plans > Our Plans

+

A person's steps are directed by the Lord.
How then can anyone understand their own way?
Proverbs 20:24, NIV

**Guest devo by Lori Skidmore
Relationship to TTF: Night to Shine volunteer and
parent of special-needs child**

The person who has to plan *everything*—that was me! You know what they say: Make your plans and hear God laugh. My second child, Turner, was born with special needs. Did I want our sweet baby to be able to do all the things a parent prays for their child? Of course! But with his limitations, I questioned if that was possible.

Throughout Turner's life, he has continued to show me that Jesus lives in him, and he continues to show those around him His love. The first time I saw this was when he made his way into a crowded room and found a woman who was hurting due to her husband's diagnosis of terminal cancer. Turner sought her out and hugged her. He has done this in countless situations.

So what I worried would be a life full of just "being" has been a life full of Jesus showing His love through a little boy who many would say has little to give to the world. If a child who is nonverbal and has too many limitations to count can reach the hurting, what can God do with *your* life? Stop trying to plan out every step and how *you* think you and those around you should be used to glorify God. Instead, take that step back, and listen to His plans. I promise they are so much better than ours.

**Spend time thanking and trusting God today that
His plans are better than your own.**

The Grand Purpose

+

"Love the Lord your God with all your heart, and with all your
soul, and with all your mind, and with all your strength." . . .
"Love your neighbor as yourself." There is no other
commandment greater than these.
Mark 12:30–31

The dictionary defines *purpose* as "the reason for which something exists or is done, made, used, etc."[2] But when it comes
to defining what our purpose is as human beings on earth, many
times the answer doesn't seem so simple.

One thing is certain: You were created for a reason. You are not
here by accident. I believe the number one reason we are on the
earth is to know our Maker, the person of God. How can we do
that? By putting into action the words of Jesus—to love God with
all our heart and to love our neighbor. This is what I call our macro
purpose.

Finding your purpose starts with knowing God through His
Son, Jesus Christ. It's also about loving your neighbor. Who is your
neighbor? Everyone you meet! Before you discover what your individual purpose is, begin to live out your macro purpose.

**How can you love God and your neighbor
well this week?**

What Is a Mission-Possible Life?

+

May the God of peace . . . equip you in every
good thing to do His will, working in us that which is
pleasing in His sight, through Jesus Christ.
Hebrews 13:20–21

Living a mission-possible life means carrying out the good works that God has already prepared for you to do. We are each on a mission to make a difference and make our lives count—a mission to help the hurting, a mission to reach the last, the lost, and the least of humanity.

When you are mission driven, you use your ability, together with God's power, to help, serve, guide, teach, pray, and lead others in your own way.

Here's a surprise for you: Your mission is not really as mysterious as you might think. Has God ever nudged your heart to take a step in a particular direction to meet a certain need? Maybe praying for or encouraging someone? Doing that is the essence of mission-possible living. Keep taking steps to do good things for the kingdom!

**What is something you feel God nudged
your heart to do?**

How Does a Mission-Possible Life Happen?

✛

I am the vine, you are the branches;
the one who remains in Me, and I in him bears much fruit,
for apart from Me you can do nothing.
John 15:5

You can live a mission-possible life because of what Jesus did for you on the cross more than two thousand years ago. This kind of life is possible only because of the sacrifice He made and the power given to Him to defeat death. When you live mission possible, you live a life that counts because of what God has done, and is doing, in and through you.

We cannot save ourselves by our good works. We receive the free gift of salvation through what Jesus has done for us on the cross. A mission-possible life happens when you do three key things:

1. Know the person of God.
2. Trust the plan of God.
3. Live out the purpose that God has for your life.

These three keys are essential for making your life count.

How can you begin to grow in your knowledge of God today?

The Great Question

✝

Who, then, is this,
that even the wind and the sea obey Him?
Mark 4:41

One of my favorite passages in the Bible is Mark 4. I think that chapter contains one of the greatest questions ever asked. Jesus finished teaching a crowd, then gathered the disciples in a boat to go over to the other side of the lake. "A great windstorm arose" (verse 37, ESV) that frightened the disciples. They woke a sleeping Jesus, and He proceeded to rebuke the winds and the seas. As the storm stopped, there was a "great calm" (verse 39, ESV). But the disciples, instead of being relieved, were filled with "great fear" (verse 41, ESV). Why were they so afraid? Many scholars believe that with this event, Jesus had performed eleven of His major miracles, confirming that He was who He claimed to be: the Son of God.

Note the sequence: a great storm, a great calm, and great fear. Now here comes the great question: "Who, then, is this, that even the wind and the sea obey Him?" (verse 41).

We must ask ourselves the same question today. I hope you can say that Jesus Christ is your Lord, Savior, Hope, Redeemer, Friend, Peace, and Love. If not, I invite you right now to choose to trust Him. He is the One who makes your mission possible.

**If you haven't accepted Jesus as your Savior,
you can say a prayer in your own words
or use the following one.**

Dear Jesus, I believe that You died on the cross and rose from the dead. I know that I am a sinner. Please come into my heart and forgive me. Thank You for trading the old for the new, the darkness for the light. Jesus, I love You and want to live for You. I give You my life. Thank You for saving me. Thank You for giving me a home in heaven, where I will live with You forever one day. Thank You for taking my place and paying my debt. In Jesus's name. Amen.

Welcome to the fam!

The Great Response

✛

Go home to your people
and report to them what great things the Lord has done
for you, and how He had mercy on you.
Mark 5:19

Yesterday, I talked about the great question "Who is Jesus?" Today, I want to talk to you about a great response to that question.

In Mark 5, the Bible tells the story of a man who had been demon possessed. He lived in a cave and cut himself with stones. One day he saw Jesus and ran toward Him. Jesus healed the man. He cast out the demons from him and sent them into a herd of pigs that ran off a cliff, into the sea. When it was time for Jesus to get back into the boat and return to the other side of the lake, the man who had been freed from the demons begged Jesus "that he might accompany Him" (verse 18). Now, that's what I call a great response!

Though the man wanted to stay with Jesus, Jesus had a different mission in mind for him. Jesus asked him to go home and tell the people there what Jesus had done for him. The man said yes, and he had an amazing impact.

God might have a different mission than what you have in mind, but whatever it is, say yes. That is the great response.

**If you already have made the decision to trust
in Jesus and would like to commit to making
your life count, go ahead and tell Him right now.
Say the following prayer with me.**

Dear Jesus, I believe I can live a mission-possible life because Your mission was accomplished. Give me courage. Remind me that because You have overcome the world, I can do whatever You have called me to do. Thank You that I get to live mission possible. Amen.

As You Go

+

As you go, preach, saying,
"The kingdom of heaven has come near."
Matthew 10:7

In the tenth chapter of Matthew, Jesus gave His twelve disciples authority to heal and cast out evil, as well as instructions on how to preach the good news. He told them to preach "as you go." I love that phrase.

As you go.

Do you know what that means? It means while living your daily life. We live out the purpose that God has for our lives by helping, serving, guiding, teaching, praying, and leading others whenever and wherever we are.

Do it as you clean up your bedroom. Do it as you hang out with your friends on a Friday night. Do it in chem lab.

Be the light Jesus has been to you, wherever you may be.

When we realize that God can use us whenever and in whatever situation, even if something seems boring or routine, the idea of living mission possible will come alive to us.

**When in the middle of an ordinary day
have you seen how God can make a difference
in someone else's life through you?**

Trust in God and His Plan

✝

Trust in the LORD with all your heart
And do not lean on your own understanding.
Proverbs 3:5

The Bible is full of heroes who were in terrible situations yet were able to live mission possible because they chose to trust in God. I think of Daniel in the lions' den. I think of Joseph, sold by his own brothers and wrongly thrown into prison. I think of Paul, who endured multiple shipwrecks, beatings, and imprisonments. I can't imagine any of them being excited during any of those circumstances. (See Daniel 6; Genesis 37; 39; and 2 Corinthians 11:23–27 to read those accounts.)

Yet here's the kicker: They trusted God. They said yes to the person of God, and they said yes to the plan of God. Why? Because they knew His character—that He is trustworthy. We can trust God because He gave His best when He gave His Son for us.

God has a great plan for your life. It may not be where you want to be in this moment, but always remember that He can use you right now, this very moment. Mission possible is where you are now, not just where you're going later.

**Do you have a hard time trusting God?
Why or why not?**

Take the Pressure Off

+

Oh, Lord God! Behold, You Yourself have made the heavens
and the earth by Your great power and by Your outstretched
arm! Nothing is too difficult for You.

Jeremiah 32:17

Though we at the foundation had been serving in anti-human-trafficking efforts for seven years, in 2020 I started to feel that we should go public with our efforts. I admit, I didn't have all the answers, nor did I have a ten-step plan. Still, I couldn't shake the feeling that God was calling me in that direction. But the more I learned about human trafficking, the more overwhelming the problem seemed. Have you ever felt a similar way?

Maybe you've found a need that has touched your heart but it feels so big that you don't know where to start. Know this: Our mission is not to end all evil or lack in this world. If it were, we would have every right to feel overwhelmed by not having the power to end every pain and hurt. Our mission is to honor God as we make a difference wherever and however we can. The outcome is up to Him.

Is there a need in the world that has touched your heart? Ask God to show you how you can help meet that need while leaving the outcome up to Him.

A Prayer of Surrender

✝

Thank You, Lord, for creating me on purpose. Search my heart and shape my desires, my motives, and my intentions to seek after You. Remind me that this life is meant for something greater than achieving success, getting rich, or accumulating likes. Forgive me when I focus on everything except You. Remind me that when I trust in You, You will guide me and Your eyes and Your hands will be upon me.

I pray each day to know You more, to know the power that raised You from the dead, and to know how You suffered because You loved me, chose me, and designed for me a life that counts. I'm so grateful for Your promise that when I seek You, I will find You. Show me Your will that I might walk in Your purpose for my life.

In Jesus's name I pray. Amen.

Based on: Psalm 139; Proverbs 8:17; Philippians 3:10; Proverbs 23:18; Psalm 32:8; Proverbs 3:5–6; 1 John 5:3

Your Mindset Matters

✛

Whatever is true, whatever is honorable, whatever is right,
whatever is pure, whatever is lovely, whatever is commendable,
if there is any excellence and if anything worthy of praise,
think about these things.
Philippians 4:8

In July 2020, researchers at Queen's University in Canada discovered that the average human brain has more than six thousand unique thoughts every single day.[3] That's a lot of thoughts!

Thoughts can be the most private and powerful parts of our human nature. No one else can know them unless we decide to share them. But thoughts can also be very destructive. Other studies have shown that up to 80 percent of our thoughts each day are negative.

We must control what goes in and out of our heads by developing the right mindset—what I describe as a particular way of thinking. In the above verse, Paul is very clear in telling us the kinds of things we should be thinking about. Next time your thoughts rage, set them straight according to the above litmus test.

Now that you're thinking about what you think about (ha ha), list three things you've been thinking about during the past thirty minutes.

A Mission M.I.N.D.S.E.T.

✛

The mind set on the flesh is death, but the mind set on
the Spirit is life and peace.
Romans 8:6

I love the word *mission*: "a task or job that someone is given to do."[4]
I believe God has sent you here for a reason, a specific mission.
Have you ever noticed that Jesus specifically commands us to love
Him with all our *minds*? Makes me wonder how often we are engaging with God in our heads. I get that a hundred things are pulling
our brains in many different directions all the time, but when we
lose focus, our mission is in jeopardy!

Everything we do starts between the ears—in our minds, with
our thoughts. I've come up with the acronym M.I.N.D.S.E.T.—a set
of mental attitudes that I will share over the next few days to help
you develop a mission-possible life:

M—Maker
I—Interruptible
N—Now
D—Different
S—Suffer
E—Excellence
T—To the End

**Before we dig in, what do you think about most
throughout your day?**

Know Your (M)aker

+

Come, let's worship and bow down,
Let's kneel before the LORD our Maker.
For He is our God,
And we are the people of His pasture
and the sheep of His hand.
Psalm 95:6–7

A mission <u>M</u>.I.N.D.S.E.T. starts by knowing your *Maker*. Just like a painting has an artist, and a skyscraper has an architect, it makes sense that the universe has a Designer. The stars in the sky. The creepy-crawlies on the ground. The schools of colorful fish in coral reefs. All things—"both in the heavens and on earth, visible and invisible"—have been created by God and for God (Colossians 1:16).

But our Creator didn't just *make* everything and take a step back. He wants to know you and use you to show His love. You don't have a real mission without knowing your *Maker*. You don't have true purpose without knowing your *Maker*. You're not going to have eternal impact without knowing your *Maker*.

A mission mindset is a God-first mindset. It starts by first recognizing where our mission came from and who it is for.

How have you experienced your Maker in your life?

Be (I)nterruptible

✛

The mind of a person plans his way,
But the Lord directs his steps.
Proverbs 16:9

I'll be the first to admit that I can get a little annoyed when things don't go as planned. But the reality is that plans change. You get a different teacher. Your parents get new jobs and you have to move. A health crisis cancels the year (or more).

But really, when does anything go 100 percent according to plan? Hardly ever. I believe there's probably going to be a change at some point in your plans. Why? Because God has a tendency to interrupt our lives.

The *I* in M.I.N.D.S.E.T. stands for *Interruptible*. Be interruptible.

Part of having a mission mindset is saying, "God, I'm okay when You interrupt my plans." It's a mindset that not only accepts change but also welcomes it. I know, crazy stuff! But remember, though a change doesn't fit your plan, it might fit God's plan.

Next time there's a hiccup in your day, instead of getting frustrated (like I have so many times), look around and see how you can make the most of the change in plans.

Ask God to give you an interruptible spirit.

Act (N)ow

+

Since his days are determined,
The number of his months is with You;
And You have set his limits so that he cannot pass.
Job 14:5

In football, the two-minute drill is a hurry-up type of offense. It's a play you use when you need to make major moves but have little time.

Life is a two-minute drill of sorts. Our clocks are ticking down. But we don't know exactly how much time we have left (see James 4:14). So we should make the most of each day.

An important part of making the most of each day is focusing on the people who are in need. I'm talking about the hurting, the abused, the abandoned, the forgotten, the hopeless, and those who don't know Jesus. We can't live on our timelines; we must live on theirs!

The N in Mission M.I.N.D.S.E.T. stands for *Now*. Don't wait until you have no choice but to take action. If God is trying to get your attention, do it *now*!

**What have you been putting off
that you know you need to get done?**

Be (D)ifferent

+

Noah was a righteous man, blameless in his generation.
Noah walked with God.
Genesis 6:9

The *D* in M.I.N.<u>D</u>.S.E.T. stands for *Different*. In Genesis 6, we get an inside look at the world after it had been cursed by God because of Adam and Eve's original sin. As humans populated the earth, wickedness was everywhere (see verse 5). The Bible tells us God was grieved that He'd made humans (see verse 6).

However, there was one man who stood out. His name was Noah. He "found favor in the eyes of the LORD" (verse 8). And because of this, God showed mercy and saved him and his family from a global flood (see 7:23).

I think that way too many times, we want to live and act like everybody else. That's the opposite of a mission mindset. A mission mindset understands that to make a difference, you have to *be different*. It doesn't care about being popular or liked. It sets aside what everyone else is doing and stands out and stands up for God. When you're willing to be a little bit different for God's glory, like Noah, watch how He can use you.

What makes you different for God?

Be Willing to (S)uffer

+

After you have suffered for a little while, the God of all grace,
who called you to His eternal glory in Christ, will Himself
perfect, confirm, strengthen, and establish you.
1 Peter 5:10

One of my favorite words in the English language is *passion*.
Today, *passion* refers to love, romance, and intense feelings.

However, digging into the word's origin brings forth an interesting discovery. The word comes from the twelfth-century Latin root
word *pati*, which means "to suffer."[5] This Latin word was used to
describe the death of Jesus on the cross. At its core, true passion is
one's willingness to suffer.

So, when you say you're passionate about something, what
you're really saying is that you care so deeply about it that you're
willing to suffer for it. This brings a whole new meaning to the
word, doesn't it?

A mission mindset embraces suffering. It's a mentality that is
willing to make sacrifices, push through pain, and fight for what
truly matters because the mission is worth it. The *S* in M.I.N.D.S.E.T.
stands for *Suffer*.

**What do you care so much about
that you're willing to suffer for it?**

Pursue (E)xcellence

+

Whether you eat or drink, or whatever you do,
do all things for the glory of God.
1 Corinthians 10:31

In 1956, twenty-seven-year-old Martin Luther King, Jr., gave a speech at a church in Montgomery, Alabama. In it, he said this about excellence:

> Whatever your life's work is, do it well.... If it falls your lot to be a street sweeper, . . . sweep streets so well that all the host of Heaven and earth will have to pause and say, "Here lived a great street sweeper, who swept his job well."[6]

What a statement! Achieving excellence is a challenge, but I believe it should always be our aim. That's why the *E* in M.I.N.D.S.E.T. stands for *Excellence*. Roughly nineteen hundred years before MLK wrote this, the apostle Paul penned something similar. He instructed the church to which he was writing to do all things for the glory of God.

We will never achieve perfection, but we can push ourselves to be our best.

How can you strive to be your best?

(T)o the End

+

Having loved His own who were in the world,
He loved them to the end.
John 13:1

The *T* in M.I.N.D.S.E.T. stands for *To the end*. Today's verse is one of my favorites. Here, Jesus finds Himself in a room in Jerusalem with His closest friends days before His arrest and crucifixion.

Jesus loved His disciples not when everything was going good. Not when He gained popularity or made a certain amount of money. No. Jesus loved . . . *to the end*. The Greek word for "the end" is *telos*. It means completion. Reaching the end goal.[7] Mission accomplished.

How did Jesus love? Until His mission was accomplished!

There were so many times Jesus could have said, "Hey, I'm out. I'm done." But He stuck with it. He went to the cross to save the world. That's *telos*. That's a mission mindset. Whatever your mission is, when God calls you to do something, do it *to the end*.

What is God asking you to complete "to the end"?

Until Practice Becomes Reflex

+

Take pains with these things; be absorbed in them,
so that your progress will be evident to all.
1 Timothy 4:15

Your brain is a remarkable machine, one that is constantly updating. This is called neuroplasticity. You can create new thought patterns by repetition, just as you can form new habits. When the neurons in your brain fire up in a certain way, it's easier for your brain to repeat that same pattern in the future.

When Paul wrote the words in 1 Timothy 4:15, he was referring to the things that, through discipline, would make his protégé Timothy a godly leader. Likely, Paul was referring to practices like reading Scripture, teaching it to others, and using spiritual gifts. Paul knew that the more Timothy worked on those important disciplines, the more they would become habits.

If you want to live mission possible, it's important to actively practice what God has instructed you to do. Sometimes He calls us to carry out actions that feel unnatural. Things like loving others when you would rather hate and being brave in the face of fear take conscious effort. Still, if you work on them enough, they will eventually become reflex.

What habits do you need to actively practice today?

Keystone Habits

✝

Only one thing is necessary; for Mary has chosen the good
part, which shall not be taken away from her.
Luke 10:42

When Paul O'Neill took his place as the new CEO of the Aluminum Company of America (Alcoa), a business that had been around for almost a century, at first people believed he could get the job done. However, the minute he started to share his plans with a roomful of investors, that confidence vanished. Instead of talking about how much money he was going to make, he stated that his top priority was the safety of Alcoa's workers. His listeners were convinced he was crazy and that he would run Alcoa into the ground.

But a year later, profits had soared. When O'Neill retired in 2000, Alcoa's annual net income was *five times* greater than before he arrived. It's quite a success story, founded on what author Charles Duhigg called a keystone habit—changing one pattern that affects different aspects of patterns. In this case, the keystone habit was safety precautions.[8]

In today's Scripture, Mary's keystone habit was choosing Jesus. When we are always about God's business, we set the stage to build better habits that help create a mission-possible life.

**Commit to a keystone habit. Set a reminder to
check in thirty days to see what other good habits
have naturally fallen into place.**

Get in Your Discomfort Zone

✛

If you know these things,
you are blessed if you do them.
John 13:17

During one of the first few weeks of my freshman year at the University of Florida, our coaches made us take ice baths for seven minutes. Ice baths are a killer method for athletic recovery. They're also *completely* not fun. Nobody wanted to get in. My teammates and I stared in fear at the freezing water, all resisting what we were going to have to do eventually. Finally, I quietly stepped aside from the crowd and crept into the tub. My toes immediately contracted. Sinking deeper, my body instinctively recoiled over and over from the freezing temperature. No lie—it was horrible, but it was a lot easier getting in the second time. And the time after that.

There are better habits to start than taking regular ice baths. The point is, get uncomfortable regularly. But don't do it just for the sake of feeling discomfort; do it with a purpose. Get uncomfortable doing things that will transform you into the person you are called to be.

**What value comes from making a habit of
being uncomfortable?**

Do It Again . . .
and Again . . . and Again

+

We have put our hope in the living God, who is the Savior of
everyone, but especially of those who have faith. This is why
we work and struggle so hard.
1 Timothy 4:10, CEV

Dr. Maxwell Maltz wrote a book called *Psycho-Cybernetics*, in which he introduced his discovery that patients take about twenty-one days to get used to seeing their new face after a plastic surgery. Over the years, that statement got twisted. Popular authors and motivational speakers dropped the *about* and started announcing what many today believe is the truth: that it takes twenty-one days to form a new habit.[9]

Although that may be true for some of us, according to a study published in the *European Journal of Social Psychology*, "it can take anywhere from 18 to 254 days for a person to form a new habit and an average of 66 days for a new behavior to become automatic."[10]

Don't get discouraged by how long good habits take to form. They are always worth the work!

**Often, the hardest part of changing a habit
is the period of transition between the old normal
and the new normal. Instead of focusing on the end
goal, divide the habit-breaking process into
smaller parts and reward yourself after
meeting each of the smaller goals.**

No Is Not Always a Bad Word

+

A prudent person foresees danger and takes precautions.
The simpleton goes blindly on and suffers the consequences.
Proverbs 27:12, NLT

In the movie *Yes Man*, Jim Carrey plays a character named Carl Allen, a man caught in a negative funk. At a self-help seminar, he's told that the secret to an amazing life is to say yes to everything. At first, the theory works and his depressing life takes an upward swing. Ultimately, however, Carl learns that saying yes all the time isn't the answer he expected.

Jesus didn't say yes to everything. Here are some instances when He said no:

- Martha asked Him to tell Mary to help her (see Luke 10:40–42).
- The crowd asked Him to stay longer (see 4:42–44).
- The scribes and Pharisees asked Him for a sign (see Matthew 12:38–39).

Not everything we say no to is necessarily wrong or sinful; it just might not be the best choice to make.

What's your process of saying yes or no to something or someone? If you can't decide whether to say yes or no to something, talk to a trusted adult (parent, mentor, teacher, pastor, counselor) and ask for wise advice.

Restrain the Rage

✠

Like a city that is broken into and without walls
So is a person who has no self-control over his spirit.
Proverbs 25:28

When's the last time rage got the best of you? Maybe you exploded on your little sister for taking something of yours without permission. Perhaps you snapped at someone who accidentally ran into you in a store or in the hall at school. And it's so easy now to let our emotions fly online—to poke fun, criticize, or belittle anyone while hiding behind a screen. After all, it's super convenient.

We are often told, "Just be yourself!" and "You do you!" I wonder if we think that means giving ourselves permission to let go of all self-control and just say whatever we want to whomever. Maybe it's time to hit pause and start to think before we speak—or post.

**Is it truly healthy to say whatever we want
and express our feelings however we want?
How does self-control fit in?**

A Prayer for Focus

✛

Thank You, Father, for loving me so much that You want me to live a significant life. Remind me each day to seek Your kingdom first and that You'll take care of the rest. As I wake up each morning, help my thoughts be in line with what You say. You are the Lord of my life, heart, soul, and mind. Forgive me when I worry too much or get distracted by silly things or even lies from the Enemy. I know that Your will for me is to stop focusing on the things of this world and focus on Your truth.

Show me the areas I need to change. Reveal the lies I have been believing that keep me stuck and distracted. Help me to be self-disciplined and remain centered on You. Remind me to be the boss of my own thoughts and think about the things that are right and good and true. Thank You for working in my life. I trust in Your plans for me.

In Jesus's name I pray. Amen.

Based on: Matthew 6:33; Ephesians 4:23–24; Romans 12:2; 1 Corinthians 9:27, 2 Corinthians 10:5; Proverbs 19:21

Created for Relationship

✝

If one can overpower him who is alone, two can resist him.
A cord of three strands is not quickly torn apart.
Ecclesiastes 4:12

One of the loneliest periods of my life was when I was traded from the Denver Broncos to the New York Jets and moved to the Northeast. I was strongly advised to stay out of the news. While trying to follow that advice, I ended up isolating myself from others. I wasn't involved in a church community. I didn't reach out much to those who were close to me. It was a pretty dark time.

Here's what I learned during that lonely season: We need one another. God made and loves relationships. He made us to be in community. He made us to live in relationship first with Him and then also with others.

Our world likes to celebrate the power of the individual, but we find that a stronger power erupts when we build and nurture a tight community. As you grow in your relationship with God, find others to travel this spiritual journey with you. We are not meant to do life alone; we are meant to grow and be like Jesus with people around us.

**How have solid friendships helped you
grow more like Jesus?**

Courageous Conversations

+

Instead, we will speak the truth in love,
growing in every way more and more like Christ,
who is the head of his body, the church.
Ephesians 4:15, NLT

G ood friends don't always tell us what we *want* to hear; instead, they share what we *need* to hear. I believe that God calls us to share truth and love with people. There have been so many times when those closest to me have had what I call "courageous conversations" with me. They've poured love and truth on me, telling me things I didn't like but needed to hear. I can't say that listening to their words was always easy or that I always received them well, but I've been influenced by these talks because I know they're coming from a place of love and truth.

As Christians, we want to grow up and mature. This might mean having courageous conversations. Don't avoid them. Instead, ask God to help you see when you need to be part of one.

Why do you think it's harmful to not speak truth to those you love and not have it spoken to you?

Shut It Down

✝

Don't use foul or abusive language. Let everything you say be good and helpful, so that your words will be an encouragement to those who hear them.

Ephesians 4:29, NLT

G rowing up, I was never a bully. I was more likely to stick up for whoever was being bullied. But one time I blew up at a church leader a few years older than me. He had a habit of talking down to younger kids. My outburst happened on a church bus, of all places. While I continue to stand behind my defense of Michael Jordan, our conversation got ugly. I think the fact that I didn't believe this guy treated us kids well bothered me more than the actual argument, but whatever the reason, I put him on blast. I got loud—*real* loud. By the time we were driving into the church parking lot, I was ashamed. I should not have been so disrespectful. I felt like I had let God down.

Tearing someone down is never a win. As Christians, we need to be sure that our words—and the attitudes behind those words—are filled with grace, kindness, and respect. Saying nothing, at times, just might be the best choice.

Have you ever said something to someone that you later regretted? What did you learn about yourself from the situation?

Tame Your Tongue

+

The tongue is a small part of the body,
and yet it boasts of great things.
See how great a forest is set aflame by such a small fire!
James 3:5

Growing up on a farm kept things interesting. I'll never forget one time the weeds had grown haywire in the pasture. My dad decided to start a controlled burn to get rid of them. We knew something had gone wrong when Dad rushed into the house, frantic. "Help! I need everyone's help!" he yelled. Our pasture was on fire! Seeing the orange and red flames licking up toward the sky, we bolted into action, beating the edges of the fire with shovels while Dad tried to douse it with a gushing garden hose.

Through the grace of God and our efforts, the fire eventually died down. Though it had burned through the weeds in our neighbor's fields, our house was untouched by the flames. Afterward, Dad used the opportunity for a teachable moment. He led us in a brief Bible study on James 3, in which we learned that just as a small spark can cause a huge fire, an uncontrolled tongue can create massive damage. Gossip. Sarcastic comments. Your words have power. Be careful how you use them.

Have you ever been gossiped about?
How does this motivate you not to do the
same to someone else?

Heart Wide Open

+

Our mouth has spoken freely to you . . . our heart is opened
wide. . . . Now in the same way in exchange—I am speaking as
to children—open wide your hearts to us, you as well.
2 Corinthians 6:11, 13

A wide-open heart, like Paul wrote about in the above passage, is *vulnerable*. That's a big word that means being okay with acknowledging and, when appropriate, sharing your true feelings or the real you.

Many times, we avoid developing deep friendships because we don't want anyone getting too close. What if they reject us or are put off by something in us they don't like? While I don't recommend becoming besties or sharing your deepest and darkest secrets with everyone you meet, you don't need to be ice cold or hold back from expressing yourself with everyone.

Think about sharing your true self so people can recognize that you are more than the cool mask you put on for school or the filtered highlights you post on social media. Don't be embarrassed to be vulnerable. Invite others, people you respect and trust, to walk alongside you when you need it most.

What is something you have tried to hide that you know should be shared with someone you trust?

Get Sharp

+

As iron sharpens iron,
So one person sharpens another.
Proverbs 27:17

Ever hear the saying "Strike while the iron is hot"? This ties in to the meaning of the ancient proverb written above. Iron requires intense heat and pressure to get sharp. Once the metal is cool, you can't use a hammer or any other object to change its shape. The iron must be reheated and struck while it's hot.

As the church, we are called to inspire each other to dig deeper into our faith and grow in maturity. We don't build a community only for entertainment or to create a cheerleading squad that agrees with everything we say. A blade will never get as sharp as possible on its own. We sharpen each other in the highs and lows of life. Sometimes we need a friend to encourage us when we're down. And sometimes we need to be that friend.

Navigating friend and family struggles is an excellent way to learn how to be more like Jesus. Think of the relationships you depend on. Let those people help you become sharper in your faith, and likewise do the same for others.

**Name three friends and write down
how each helps you grow as a person.**

Get It Together

+

How good and pleasant it is
when God's people live together in unity!
Psalm 133:1, NIV

During one memorable Tebow vacation, we siblings, our parents, and some friends participated in a beach Olympics event. Whether we were playing *Minesweeper,* competing in tug-of-war, or wrangling a snake—yes, we actually did that—I made sure we started our morning with an adrenaline rush. But soon our competitive natures got the better of us. Arguments exploded. What should have been a fun time turned tense.

Then another family at the resort asked to compete against us. Whatever beefs we Tebows had with each other were instantly quashed. We locked in and rallied strong and won every game we played against them.

How did that happen? How did we shift our family atmosphere from competitive fury to cheering each other on? We Tebows finally got on the same page. We found a common purpose to believe in and fight for.

I know at times believers seem more divided than united. When this happens at church or in your group of friends, remind yourself that we are not supposed to be fighting each other. We must unite to love and serve God and others and make His glory known.

**Have you ever worked together with another
Christian who may have had different opinions
than you? What was the result?**

Lead to Serve

+

Whoever wants to become prominent among you
shall be your servant.
Matthew 20:26

According to Matthew 20, as Jesus got closer to His death, He laid out for His disciples what would happen. He talked about being handed over to the religious leaders, condemned to death, beaten and crucified, and finally resurrected. At some point after this, the mother of two disciples, James and John, rushed to Jesus with both sons in tow. She could have asked Jesus a million questions at that point. What she chose to say is baffling.

"Um, so can my boys, like, sit right beside you, uh, in heaven?" (see verse 21).

I love how Jesus responds: "You do not know what you are asking" (verse 22).

I bet He would say the same for those of us who desire glory or all the attention. Jesus calls us to servanthood. He came to earth to give His life as a ransom for our sins. That's ultimate service. And He expects the same from us. Service isn't something that's just for those who are less than. It is required of the greatest.

**How can you serve someone today regardless
of whether they (or others) will ever find out?**

Preparation for the Purpose

✝

Say to the people of Israel: "I am the LORD.
I will free you from your oppression and will rescue you from
your slavery in Egypt. I will redeem you with a powerful
arm and great acts of judgment."
Exodus 6:6, NLT

B orn into slavery and slowed by a speech disorder, Moses seemed an unlikely candidate to lead an entire nation to freedom. In fact, when the Lord commanded him to speak up against the most powerful ruler in the land, Moses resisted. He believed he was a no-body.

However, in God's eyes, Moses was anything but a nobody. Even though he didn't know it at the time, his entire life up to that point had prepared him to answer God's call. During the forty years of his life as a shepherd in the wilderness, God was preparing Moses to shepherd the nation of Israel out of slavery and into the Prom-ised Land.

None of us knows what God is doing behind the scenes. Be all in, whatever you are doing. You have no idea how He is going to use your experience as preparation for a greater purpose.

**You know that situation in your life right now
that makes you feel small and insignificant?
Ask God to help you choose an all-in attitude
about it and persevere.**

No Small Role

+

*The one who is faithful in a very little thing is also faithful
in much; and the one who is unrighteous in a very little thing
is also unrighteous in much.*
Luke 16:10

M oses was called to lead the nation of Israel out of Egyptian slavery, but he wasn't left to do it alone.

After the Israelites left Egypt, during a battle with the Amalekites, God dished out to Moses an interesting strategy. As long as Moses held his hands up, the Israelites kept winning the battle. When his hands came down, the Amalekites started winning. The Bible doesn't tell us how long the battle went, but at some point his hands grew heavy. So his brother, Aaron, and another elder, named Hur, stood on each side of Moses and helped prop up their leader's arms so Israel could claim the victory. With their help, his arms remained steady for the rest of the battle.

God may call you to a mission in which you'll have to fight or pray or hold up those who are carrying a heavy weight. These jobs are all equally important. Be faithful in whatever you are called to do.

**Pray for God to open your eyes to whatever
He has called you to, great or small.**

The Art of Staying Grounded

+

The LORD gave and the LORD has taken away.
Blessed be the name of the LORD.
Job 1:21

Massive changes to our daily lives and tragedies in the news or in our own families or friend groups have made many of us more anxious than we've ever been. How can we feel settled when our world is rocked with tragedy and chaos?

One way to stay grounded is to live with open hearts, knowing that whatever we have belongs not to us but to God. He gave it to us, and He can take it back.

Some of us live like we have control over everything. We tightly grip our time, our love, our talents, and our resources, yet all we can really do is focus on today. Right now. This moment.

When we live this way, our fingers uncurl. Our hearts open. We begin to live with open minds and open spirits. And when we do, we become willing to step out in faith in order to allow God to take us where He wants us to go and do the things He wants us to do.

Do you live as though what you have belongs to you or to God? What needs to change?

Do What's Necessary

✝

When you eat the fruit of the labor of your hands,
You will be happy and it will go well for you.
Psalm 128:2

A mission-possible life is lived every day—at practice and in the championship game, in rehearsal and during the performance. Just as important as game day are the practices and training put in on all the other days of the week. In fact, the tip-off matters more when each day of the week you attacked your drills for hours, even when no one was watching.

Living a mission-possible life is about loving and serving God and others. It's not about performing Tom Cruise–like stunts that defy gravity and impress the masses. It's doing what's necessary to move the mission forward. This looks different for different people and at different times. It can mean coming up with a consistent schedule of praying and reading the Bible. It could mean studying more than playing or taking control of certain habits that aren't the best for you. Maybe it means loving others when it's really hard. The grind may not be exciting at times, but there is power in the details.

It is tempting to focus your attention on the goal or end result. Instead, pay attention to the steps you'll have to take on the road to your goal. List three things that will help get you there.

Grace Within the Grind

✝

By grace you have been saved through faith; and this is not
of yourselves, it is the gift of God; not a result of works,
so that no one may boast.
Ephesians 2:8–9

D*o whatever it takes. Hustle hard.* These are great motivational quotes and hashtags. I'm all about working hard for a purpose. We can't shy away from responsibility. Work hard? Absolutely! In fact, work as if the miracle depends on you. But know, and have faith, that the miracle will happen because of God.

When the stress piles up and you're tossing and turning in bed more than snoozing or if you find yourself constantly comparing your efforts to someone else's, take a breath. Remember, you're not in this alone. Turn your attention to the center of it all: Jesus Christ. With Him, you have everything, including the grace you need to step away from the grind.

**Write down a list of what you have to do today
or this week. Now take that list, cover it with
your hand, and pray over it. Ask God for the
strength you will need to get done what
He wants you to get done.**

Break It Up

✝

Behold, I am going to do something new.
Isaiah 43:19

Sometimes the things we need to do daily become, well, boring. Make the bed. Complete homework. Study. Practice. They're important. We need to do them. Yet doing the same thing over and over, day after day, can become a dry routine. This can also be true of our spiritual lives. Reading a devo every morning sounds good on Day 1, but on Day 47, it might start to get boring.

A Christian author named A. W. Tozer wrote a book titled *Rut, Rot, or Revival*. In it, he taught how churches can get unstuck from the drudgery of the routine, which he called the enemy of the church today, and expect a fresh touch from God. Have you ever found yourself so overwhelmed that your spiritual life takes a back seat? My advice? Interrupt yourself.

There's no need to do anything crazy or overcomplicate things. Just shake things up a bit. When you read a Bible verse, pause to soak it in. Or if you don't normally listen to worship music, try it. Or pray while taking a walk. Routines are important, but sometimes they need to be interrupted on purpose.

How can you mix up your time with God today?

True Joy Comes from God

✝

The joy of the LORD is your strength.
Nehemiah 8:10, NIV

Guest devo by Jennifer Dobson
Relationship to TTF: adoption-grant recipient

Our daughters have every reason to be angry. We have turned their lives upside down with the choices we have made—choices to follow Jesus into a future unknown to them both. Our older daughter carried the weight of a seven-year journey to bring her adopted sister home. Our youngest has learned to come to terms with the future she has been given: leaving her birth country behind and learning to trust, let go, live in a biracial family, and believe that unconditional love does not quit. On top of all that, she is also in a wheelchair.

Socks make me want to cry. To watch our youngest daughter struggle to put socks on her feet, feet that fail her, breaks my heart. It is the little things that threaten to steal my joy. Little things, like socks, should steal her joy, yet they do not. Spend five minutes with her and you will experience her belly laugh. She has an infectious personality that Jesus deposited deep into her soul that no messy journey could overtake. Her joy explodes despite all the obstacles she has faced. She has a joy that is supernatural, from a supernatural God. She has a joy that changes people—a joy that makes others take note that something is different. Most days, instead of being angry and frustrated with her socks, she breaks out in song, "Mom, will you help me put on my socks?"

Where does your joy come from?

A Prayer for Community

✝

Dear Lord, thank You for creating me to be in relationship with You and others. Help me to be the friend I want to have. Forgive me for falling short in my relationships. Where I have failed to forgive, show mercy, and be just and fair. Help me to be kind, humble, gentle, and patient. Help me to freely forgive others as You forgive me. Teach me how to love others the way You love them and the way You love me when I am unlovable. You know the struggles I have in my relationships. Give me a soft heart and a wise mind to work through those challenges.

Help me to be faithful in the little things. I thank You for giving me the ability to do the tasks put before me. Remind me of Your purpose. I give today, and each day, to You. Thank You for ordering my steps.

In Jesus's name I pray. Amen.

Based on: Colossians 3:12–13; Ephesians 4:32; 1 John 4:20–21; Luke 16:10; Psalm 119:133

Created to Feel

✝

A time to weep and a time to laugh;
A time to mourn and a time to dance.
Ecclesiastes 3:4

Have you ever been caught off guard by a wave of emotion that came out of nowhere? Maybe you found yourself turning green when a friend told you how she aced the test that she barely studied for—the one you crammed for all night but flopped? Someone else's good news can sometimes throw you for a loop and bring out an ugly side.

Feeling is human. It's natural. While it is dangerous to let negative feelings like bitterness and envy take root in our lives, we don't have to be afraid of them. We can sit with and process them.

God created us with feelings. That awe you feel when watching the sun go down in a pool of gold and orange colors. The feeling of joy you get when you spend time with a friend you haven't seen in a while. Our emotions are gifts from God. There is a time to feel each one of them.

**What do you feel today?
Take a moment to reflect on this.**

Jesus Felt Things Too

✝

We do not have a high priest
who cannot sympathize with our weaknesses.
Hebrews 4:15

God is able to handle our emotions so well because He knows what it's like to have them. The writer of Hebrews reminds us that we have a High Priest—Jesus—who is able to sympathize with us. This means He knows what we feel.

In Matthew 21, when the religious leaders allowed the temple of God to be used as a marketplace instead of a house of prayer, Jesus flipped tables to show His righteous anger. The Bible tells us that though Jesus taught and healed crowds of people, He would also get weary and need to slip away by Himself to pray (see Luke 5:16). And though He was all powerful and fully aware of how the story would end, He wept with the others at the tomb of Lazarus (see John 11:35).

Jesus understands our feelings because He felt them too. He doesn't look down on our pitiful nature or condemn us for whatever emotions overwhelm us. He comes beside us and helps us through them because He understands.

**How does knowing that Jesus experienced
emotions affect your relationship with Him today?**

The Strength of Convictions

✝

Jesus Christ is the same yesterday and today, and forever.
Hebrews 13:8

According to pastor and author David Jeremiah, *conviction* is "a fixed belief, a deeply held set of certainties that lodges in the center of your mind and heart."[11] Convictions are not opinions that you form on the spot, nor do they change depending on your mood or whom you are talking to. You do not choose your convictions without taking time to really think about them.

We intentionally form our convictions over time and let them shape or reshape our perspective. Our convictions keep us focused on our goals even when we don't feel like working for them.

When your convictions are rooted in whose you are and living a mission-possible life, they will drive you toward your calling. As believers, our convictions must rest in who God is and who He says we are. We can trust that Jesus is the same yesterday, today, and forever. This can be our unchanging, steady conviction. When we live based on the Word of God—Jesus—we can remain steady, even when our emotions or circumstances try to shake us.

Write down three of your convictions.

You Have a Choice

+

When [Jesus] came ashore, He saw a large crowd, and felt
compassion for them and healed their sick.
Matthew 14:14

When Jesus received the devastating news that His cousin John the Baptist had been killed, He wanted to get away and be by Himself. He was terribly sad, and He had every right to mourn the loss of His cousin in private.

But while Jesus was going to the mountain to be alone, a crowd followed Him. At that point in His ministry, they were just getting to know who He was, and they wanted to know more. And He set aside His need and began to encourage them. I don't know if I would have done that!

Sometimes you may have some tough emotions that you have every right to feel. It may be tempting to retreat. And it's okay to take a break and get any help you may need. But may you follow the example Jesus left us and continue pursuing your mission. When you willingly follow where He leads, you allow Him to work through your obedience. You may be surprised how God uses you in those moments.

**How can you lay aside what you feel today
and pursue your God-given mission?**

Your Emotions Can Be a Weapon Against You

✝

Be of sober spirit, be on the alert. Your adversary, the devil,
prowls around like a roaring lion, seeking someone to devour.
1 Peter 5:8

When a lioness hunts her prey, she lurks in the background, quietly observing and assessing the weakness of her target as she slowly glides toward it. Then, at just the right moment, she makes her move and attacks.

We have an adversary who prowls like a lioness planning her attack. Satan's aim is to distract us from living mission-possible lives, often with hardship and pain. We can get caught up in sadness or heartbreak and stop believing that God still has a plan and purpose for our lives. It's important to acknowledge and deal with our feelings, but when we focus on only our emotions instead of living the lives we are called to live, we are ultimately focused on ourselves instead of on Christ. If the Enemy can get us distracted from our purpose and our God, then he can weaken and attack us. He can keep us from our mission-possible lives.

Keep your eyes on Jesus, even when your emotions try to convince you not to.

**Do you control your emotions, or do they
control you? What feelings do you need to
hand over to God today?**

When You Don't Feel Like It

✝

The heart is more deceitful than all else
And is desperately sick;
Who can understand it?
Jeremiah 17:9

S ome days, you wake up ready to crush life. The sky is blue, the sun is warm, and you feel your best. Living a mission-possible life is easy when you feel like that.

Other days, though, you don't feel that way. Exhaustion takes over. Fear creeps in. Worry tangles up inside your mind. It feels like the weight of the world rests on your shoulders. The Bible tells us that the heart is the most deceitful thing there is. We can feel our emotions, but can we always trust them? When emotions take over, we have two choices: soak in our misery or turn our feelings over to God.

Our emotions should never be our guide for how we decide to live each day. Feelings come and go and change with the weather. Thankfully, we have a Savior who does understand our heart, as deceitful as it is. Make the choice today to immediately stop basing your choices and actions on whatever you feel and take it to God instead.

**Are your feelings getting in the way of
living out your mission? How can you trust God
with those feelings instead?**

Bring Your Worst

✝

Come to Me, all who are weary and burdened,
and I will give you rest.
Matthew 11:28

When emotions overwhelm you and you're not sure how to press on in conviction, go back to the Source. We can bring everything to Jesus, including our worst. He can handle our pain, our hurt, even our tantrums.

Sometimes the heavy burdens that weigh down your heart make it feel impossible to live from a place of conviction. The emotions you carry can drain you to the point that all you have to offer Jesus is a half-hearted prayer. It's okay—whatever you have, it's enough for Jesus.

Certain feelings are too big to manage on your own, and in those moments, you don't have to pretend to be strong. Jesus promises to give you rest in exchange for your burdens. Instead of sadness, He will give you joy. Instead of despair, He will give you hope. Instead of anger, He will give you a soft heart. Jesus will always take the burdens that weigh you down and give you the rest you need, because He loves you.

Running your race is so much easier without a heavy load on your back. If you feel too weak today to work through what you feel, lay it all before Jesus.

**Are you overwhelmed by your emotions?
How can you lay down your burdens?**

An Audience of One

✝

Whatever you do, do your work heartily,
as for the Lord and not for people.
Colossians 3:23

During college and early in my professional career, sometimes I felt crushing pressure to perform at my best. I've since gained a new perspective. I've come to realize that winning the trophy is not what matters most.

More than achieving success in this world, I want to be a believer—first and foremost, a believer in God. I also want to be a believer in the people around me and a believer in why we're all here. A believer who, more than anything else, is working for the Lord and serving His purposes.

Remember that whatever you do, your main audience is God, not others. That's why, in the book of Colossians, the apostle Paul reminds us to live life *for* the Lord. In other words, live with God's purposes in mind. As humans, we tend to want to highlight our efforts, but it's not likes or high fives that deserve our energy. We need the love of our Father in heaven. Live each day performing in front of an audience of one: God. It's His attention and approval that matter most.

**What would your life be like if you lived for
an audience of God alone instead of trying to
impress the people around you?**

Be You

✝

I will give thanks to You, because I am awesomely
and wonderfully made;
Wonderful are Your works,
And my soul knows it very well.
Psalm 139:14

When I talk about how special each one of us is, I'm not talking about the way society sees us. We are not special because we attend fancy schools, are on championship sports teams, or have the most friends.

I'm talking about the uniqueness with which we were created—the innate gifts, talents, and abilities that make up who we are. Think about what you love to do. Think about what you're good at, the unique traits that are hardwired in you. Maybe you are a talented musician or athlete. You may have a unique way of teaching others or great communication skills. You may be compassionate or charismatic. You might be a strategic thinker, skilled at building things, or creative.

We all have trouble accepting the parts of ourselves that we don't like: perhaps our natural hair color or texture, the shape and size of our bodies, or our family dynamics. Many of us get stuck in life because we compare ourselves to others and feel less than. Instead of wanting to be like someone else, make the most of your own talents. Use whatever God has given you.

List three things about you that are unique.

Whose You Are

+

I have set the LORD continually before me;
Because He is at my right hand, I will not be shaken.
Psalm 16:8

I know what it feels like to be adored, praised, and respected. I also know what it feels like to be criticized, made fun of, and fired. One of the greatest things I've learned is that neither the highs nor the lows in life define who I am. The same is true for you.

Our lives are going to be filled with successes and failures, wins and losses. And although our feelings may change, one thing must remain steady: our identities. Our identities are shaped by our experiences, our backgrounds, culture, media, and our communities.

Who we are is more important than what we do or even what happens to us. Our identities are tied to whose we are.

I am a child of God. My identity is grounded in my faith in a God who loves me, who gives me purpose, who sees the big picture, and who always has a greater plan.

When you have this identity that's bigger than what you do or have, every time someone says you're not good enough or that you can't or you won't or you shouldn't, you can still overcome.

**Write down a high and a low you've experienced.
Then try to imagine how the truth that you are
a child of God can help you process both.**

The Object of God's Love

✝

This is real love—not that we loved God, but that he loved us
and sent his Son as a sacrifice to take away our sins.
1 John 4:10, NLT

Feeling loved is a cozy emotion bundled in warmth and comfort. It's also an emotion that typically comes because of something we have done or said or what we offer to another person. Your coach might love you because you score touchdowns. Your schoolmates might love you because you're the quarterback of the football team. Your friend might love you because you've got the best clothes and always share.

But would they die for you? Would they give up their lives so that you could live? That's what Jesus did!

Knowing you are the object of God's love lays the groundwork for who you are. He loves you as an individual, just because He does. You are wanted. You are adopted into His family. You belong. Who you are is not based on what others say or think about you, on fitting in, on belonging to a certain crowd, or on what kind of job you do. Your identity is based on belonging to God. And no one can take this foundation away from you.

**Think of a time when you hungered for belonging.
Write down how it feels to know that you
already belong in the family of God.**

A Match Made in Heaven

✝

*To Him who is able to do far more abundantly beyond all that
we ask or think, according to the power that works within us.*
Ephesians 3:20

We get to live mission possible not because of how great we are or what we have to offer but because of who makes the mission possible.

You are not a mistake. You were created and put on this earth for a reason. The God of this universe says that He has good works for you to accomplish (see Ephesians 2:10). You might feel that you don't have that much to offer. Yes, you do. You might not realize it, but you plus Jesus equals miracles.

Jesus once fed a crowd of more than five thousand people five fish and two loaves of bread. The simple lunch was given to His disciples by a little boy who was willing to trust Jesus with all he had, which really wasn't much. If you don't know the story, Jesus performed a miracle and fed every person in attendance that day—and there were leftovers (see Matthew 14:13–21)!

A mission-possible life doesn't depend on you. The miracle of living that way depends on God. Trust Him and give Him all you have, and see what He can do with it!

**What's the most humanly impossible thing
you will ask God to do today?**

You Are God's Child

✝

You are all sons and daughters of God
through faith in Christ Jesus.
Galatians 3:26

A few years ago, I wrote a book called *Shaken: Discovering Your True Identity in the Midst of Life's Storms.* I got some flak for the title. "No," the publisher said. "It's too negative. How about *Unshaken?*" I get where they were coming from. They wanted a title that illustrated the strength and steadfastness of faith. But at that particular time in my life, everything around me felt shaken. I was holding on to a dream I believed was from God, yet I was facing one closed door after another. The space between the highs and the lows was extreme. I felt confused. The title perfectly reflected the state of my emotions and circumstances. *Shaken* it was.

That time in my life also forced me to recognize and remind myself of my identity in Christ. I had to remember that no matter what my emotions are saying or what is happening around me, who I am and whose I am is always secure. That part of me is anchored in the God who created me. Because you're a believer, nothing will change your status as an adopted son or daughter into the family of your Father in heaven.

**When you feel shaken in your faith, what is one
truth you can hold on to?**

The Object of Our Faith

✝

We have peace with God through our Lord Jesus Christ,
through whom we also have obtained our introduction by faith
into this grace in which we stand.
Romans 5:1–2

"Faith over fear" is a slogan you see everywhere, from T-shirts to face masks to hashtags. It's an important, biblical truth. But there's a greater truth to that catchy statement. It's not so much that faith itself overcomes; it's the One we have faith in who overcomes, and that's Jesus. I can have faith—faith in other people, faith in a robust economy, faith in outward confidence—but all those things fall short of the unchanging omnipotence of Jesus.

God helps us overcome not only fear but insecurity, confusion, doubt, pain, and dysfunction. As believers, we are connected to not only the Source of life but also Life itself.

The only way to strengthen your identity in whose you are is to deepen your relationship with Him. Don't just read books about the Bible; *read the Bible.* Don't just listen to podcasts about prayer; *pray.* Don't just immerse yourself in surfacy interactions; *surround yourself* with people who encourage and tell you the truth, even when you don't want to hear it. Don't just fill your mind with positive affirmations; *fix your eyes* on the One who gave His life for you and trampled death and is coming back one day.

**What's one thing you can do today to deepen
your relationship with Jesus?**

A Prayer for Grounding

✝

Lord, forgive me when I have put my faith and trust in earthly things or my own achievements or skills. I want to build a heart, mind, and soul that honor and delight in Your ways. Thank You for being the anchor in my life that keeps me strong and steady. I know that with You by my side, I will not be shaken. As a believer in Jesus Christ, I am a child of God, connected to the very life of Your Son. He sustains my life. I am so sorry for the times I take for granted who You have created me to be. When I complain about what I have or what I don't have, remind me that I am fearfully and wonderfully made. Settle these truths into my heart so my soul knows it well.

When my emotions overwhelm me, may Your convictions lead me. I pray the peace of Jesus Christ rules in my heart and leads me with wisdom to make the right decisions. Thank You that no matter the chaos that surrounds me, You will help me stand steady and persevere in doing Your work.

In Jesus's name I pray. Amen.

Based on: Proverbs 23:26; Psalm 16:8; John 1:12; 15:5; Psalm 139:14; Colossians 3:15; 1 Corinthians 15:58

Give It Up to Be Free

✢

It was for freedom that Christ set us free.
Galatians 5:1

For Christians, freedom is a paradox, something that doesn't seem to make sense. It's a gift you get only when you surrender, giving everything to God—who first gave everything to you. It's a radical trust, one not built upon the lesser things that this world offers but instead rooted in the only One who truly satisfies all our needs and longings.

Surrender can sound like a negative word. At face value, the word makes us think of negative images of waving a white flag and admitting defeat. Surrender seems like something we should avoid at all costs.

Biblically, however, you must embrace surrender. To live a mission-possible life, you must have your priorities in order. The first step involves surrendering your life, your wants, your preferences, and even your actions to God. Then, at this crossroads of acceptance and surrender, you will be able to wholeheartedly ask God to use you for His purposes, no matter your strengths or weaknesses.

How does the truth that surrender leads to freedom help you live a mission-possible life?

Free to Hope

✝

May the God of hope fill you with all joy
and peace in believing, so that you will abound in hope
by the power of the Holy Spirit.
Romans 15:13

For many people around the world in the past few years, hope has been hard to find. Yet if Jesus has truly set us free, hope is already ours, both to give and receive. This is not to say we won't experience hard times. Of course we will! The Bible even tells us this. However, hope that is born out of the freedom Jesus offers is never lost. He who promised is faithful. We don't have to wonder if He will come through. We may not know when, where, or how. But we can know, deep in our souls, that He will—somehow, some way.

What happens when we are filled with hope? God becomes more real in our lives because we become more dependent on Him. If you think about it, surrendering to Him is powerful! In a world of uncertainty, that is something we ought to strive for.

**Do you know someone who is caught in
a seemingly hopeless situation? Is there a way you
can share hope with them today?**

Jesus, the Master of Surrender

+

Being found in appearance as a man,
He humbled Himself by becoming obedient to
the point of death: death on a cross.
Philippians 2:8

From the big screens to our tablet and phone screens, we live in a society that tells us to look out for number one. It's all about *us*. If we don't take care of ourselves first, who will? To the nonbeliever, a life surrendered to God and others doesn't make much sense.

If anyone had both reason and ability to look out for number one, it was Jesus. He was the Son of God. Instead, He did the very opposite: He lived a life of sacrifice for others. And in what would become the single greatest act of service the world would ever know, He humbled Himself by becoming obedient to the point of death.

We will probably never be asked to die in another person's place. However, those of us who know Him will be called countless times to put others' needs above our own. We will find that there is freedom in putting others first.

Think of someone you can serve today, and do it.

Purpose over Preference

+

Give me your heart . . .
And let your eyes delight in my ways.
Proverbs 23:26

When I was a teenager, the summers offered me a couple of options. One of them was extra athletic training that could give me an edge over the other kids the following football season. Another opportunity was spending a few weeks on a mission trip in the Philippines serving people and sharing the good news. While I'd have rather trained than served, I knew what would bring me a greater purpose.

A mission-possible life has less to do with us and more to do with others. It requires submitting our preferences to God. Sometimes that doesn't feel very good or doesn't make you look as good as you'd like. This is where trusting Him is so important. If you've made the decision to trust Him, He both gives you the mission and makes it possible. Trust that He's got better plans for your life than you do.

Surrendering what we prefer to God may not come easy, but when we do, it'll always be worth it.

How can you make God's purpose for your life a priority over your own needs?

Say Yes

✝

Your kingdom come.
Your will be done.
Matthew 6:10

I'll never forget the day my dad called me from overseas and told me that he had just purchased the freedom of four young girls who were about to be sold into slavery. Now he needed the foundation to help the girls so they wouldn't fall into danger again.

There's a saying that evil triumphs when good men do nothing. My dad was not going to be the man who did nothing. Had he not acted, who knows what terrible things would have happened to those four girls?

Honestly, we at the foundation weren't prepared. But that moment—a moment in which my dad took a stand for what was right—was the beginning of a ripple effect still in motion today. Through the years, our work to fight against human trafficking and commitment to bringing freedom to the enslaved has grown stronger.

We might not know the how or the why involved in the process, but what's most important in the moment is taking the first step: saying yes.

**Is there something God is asking you to do?
Take a moment to decide the first step you need
to take to say yes.**

Yes = Impact

✝

Our life for yours if you do not tell this business of ours; and it shall come about when the LORD gives us the land that we will deal kindly and faithfully with you.
Joshua 2:14

In the Bible, Rahab was a Canaanite woman from Jericho who hid two Israelite spies in her home (see Joshua 2). She could have been killed for doing so, but she trusted God. And in the process, she saved the spies as well as her entire family.

We know nothing about Rahab's life prior to this time. But from the information the Bible does give about her, it's likely that she was looked down upon as a woman living on the very bottom rung of society's ladder. Yet God did not see her that way. He saw a woman who was strong and brave enough to say yes to His plan, despite the danger it entailed.

Maybe you relate to Rahab. Let her story remind you that God can, and will, use anyone to accomplish His will and play a significant role in His mission.

True, our yes to God may come with a cost, but the impact is always worth the cost. Think back to a time your yes made a positive difference.

Give God Your Pain

+

God causes all things to work together for good to those who
love God, to those who are called according to His purpose.
Romans 8:28

Not every prayer is answered in the way that we want. Sometimes things happen for reasons we can't explain, that don't make sense, or that seem unfair. One of my favorite quotes is from my big sister Christy. Amid her health struggles and the challenges of being a missionary overseas, she would always tell me, "God will never waste pain that's offered to Him." I love that.

God will never waste your pain. He will never waste your heartache. He will never waste your loss. He can, and will, use even the bad in order to make something good.

I know it's easier to hold on to the bad stuff and keep God out of the picture. But when we do, we're the ones who suffer. Trust God. Trust that He loves you and has a plan. Yes, even for your pain.

**What hurt are you struggling with right now
that you need to surrender to God?
Make the decision to do it today.**

God's Hands and Feet

+

As God's chosen people, holy and dearly loved,
clothe yourselves with compassion, kindness, humility,
gentleness and patience.
Colossians 3:12, NIV

Guest devo by Kelli Smith
Relationship to TTF: mother of W15H recipient

We often hear that we should be the hands and feet of Christ, but what does that look like? During our seven-year cancer battle followed by starting a new life without my sweet son, Chase, I have relied heavily on my Father in heaven's "earthly" hands and feet.

So many people in our tiny school, small town, large state, and social media presence have extended their hands and feet to show us compassion and God's love. God continually sent an "earthly" physical dose of His grace and reassurance. He would send someone clothed in kindness and humility who had a gentle, empathetic ear to listen to our heartbreak and wipe away our tears.

The compassion that Christ pours out through our family, friends, and strangers is such a gift! I am so thankful for others who are willing to be God's hands and feet.

How can you make a difference as the "earthly" hands and feet for Christ?

Keep Taking the Loop

✝

Be strong and do not lose courage,
for there is a reward for your work.
2 Chronicles 15:7

D o you ever feel God nudging your heart to do something—talk to someone or send a friend a message? I'll never forget being in downtown Austin one evening with some friends. On our way home after dinner, stopped at a traffic light, I saw a homeless man on the sidewalk. I felt an inner pull to park the car and go talk to him. I chose not to, but God's nudging was too powerful and I returned to downtown not long after.

I drove around, taking the same loop around the city streets multiple times in my effort to find the guy. About the fourth time I looped around, I happened upon a random side street where homeless people were gathered. I took the opportunity to pass out water and encourage some people.

I believe God speaks to us in our hearts more than we realize. Don't be discouraged when you feel you've missed an opportunity He has presented. Keep taking the loop. It's never too late.

When was the last time you felt God speaking to your heart? What did you do about it?

Do It Anyway

✝

Be strong and courageous, do not be afraid or in
dread of them, for the LORD your God is the One who is going
with you. He will not desert you or abandon you.
Deuteronomy 31:6

Every now and then, I still get nervous about speaking in public, even though I've done it for years. It's because I care about the outcome. I want to do my best for God and for everyone who is listening. When we do something that stretches who we are, that demands courage, that pulls us into unfamiliar territory, it's going to be worth it. Still, that first step is always the hardest.

When is the last time you did something outside your comfort zone? Something that wasn't familiar but could do a lot of good in the life of another? When you remain in your comfort zone, you don't grow. You're not challenged. You stay the same.

It's okay to feel afraid while taking the first step. Doing something against the flow of your friends, society, or the crowd might tempt you to run and hide.

Don't fight against what's right or what's possible because the unknown territory freaks you out. Do it anyway.

Write down a prayer for courage.

Do What You Love and Has Meaning

✛

I have seen that nothing is better than when a person
is happy in his activities, for that is his lot.
Ecclesiastes 3:22

I don't do things that I don't care about. I don't endorse brands I don't care for. I want to do things that I love, that I'm passionate about, that matter. I want to do things that have significance. For example, I love playing sports, writing, and motivating others, but what's most significant for me is to bring faith, hope, and love to those needing a brighter day during their darkest hour. Choosing to do the things that are significant is what drives me most of all. Happiness can come in many ways, but fulfillment is always attached to a deeper purpose.

Fulfillment and significance will come only when we do what makes us happy *together with* a greater purpose. Find a mission and believe in it. When you believe in the mission, you will be willing to sacrifice and embrace the grind that comes with it.

**What is one thing that you enjoy doing
that is also something through which you can
serve and love others?**

No Bossing Around

✝

We are taking every thought captive to
the obedience of Christ.
2 Corinthians 10:5

It's not easy to hear others say bad things about us. But sometimes the harshest words we hear come from our own minds. Think about some negative things you've thought about yourself over the past week, or even in the last twenty-four hours.

- *I won't get the part.*
- *I'll never be able to make the team.*
- *I'm not smart enough for this class.*

Negative thoughts usually lead to more negative thoughts.

I love the intentionality with which Paul wrote this verse: "We are taking every thought captive." It's almost aggressive. In other words, "I'm not going to let these thoughts boss me around."

When was the last time you allowed negative thoughts to take you prisoner? I'm sure the outcome wasn't a good one. When poisonous thoughts seep into your mind and try to get comfortable, buck up. Remember the One who is really in charge. If the winds and waves obey Him, your thoughts can too.

What is at the center of your thought life?

Represent

✝

We are ambassadors for Christ, as though God
were making an appeal through us; we beg you on behalf
of Christ, be reconciled to God.
2 Corinthians 5:20

If you're creating awareness for a hair-product company, shaving your head probably isn't the first task you ought to assign yourself two weeks after signing the contract. That would be some sketchy ambassador behavior. What you should do is tell everyone about how your morning shampoo smelled incredible and made your hair super shiny.

The dictionary defines the word *ambassador* as "an authorized messenger or representative."[12] I represent a few different companies, and part of the requirement of those relationships is to fulfill certain contractual obligations. A contract says, "If . . . then." In other words, "*If* I do a, b, and c, *then* you will do x, y, and z." I'm grateful I'm not in a contractual relationship with God. As believers, we are in *covenant*—a promise—with God, who says, "I will," regardless of our actions. He promises to love us even if we fail Him.

It's an honor to be called an ambassador for Christ. May the greatest thing we do be to show off Jesus. May we live in such a way that others want in on this kind of life.

What is your goal in being an ambassador for Jesus?

Fear Not

✝

Fear not, for I am with you;
Be not dismayed, for I am your God.
I will strengthen you,
Yes, I will help you,
I will uphold you with My righteous right hand.
Isaiah 41:10, NKJV

Guest devo by Elise Lato
Relationship to TTF: mother of W15H recipient
who passed away from neurofibromatosis

I have always struggled with fear. When I was little, I was afraid of the dark. When I got a little older, my fear of the dark morphed into fears of conflict, decisions, my future. There are times that fear has been good, and times where it has held me back.

During our hardest time, our eldest daughter, Alexis, chose Isaiah 41:10 to be her inspiration to guide her through her journey and, most of all, find comfort and love. When we were told Alexis was terminally ill, all my other fears seemed so little compared to the new fear I never knew I would have to face: the fear of losing my child. How would I survive daily with part of my life and heart in heaven and the rest here on earth?

Now I look back and see that fear wasn't always a bad thing. It has challenged me, sometimes making me stop everything to think about and face it. And I'm so grateful that fear has made me really depend on God for answers, for strength, and sometimes even for comfort.

Make a list of the fears you are currently battling
with, then talk to Jesus about each one.

A Prayer to Strive Well

+

Lord, there are times I haven't been the greatest ambassador for You. I put my desires, my preferences, and my need to look good and be right over Your truth and what You value. Forgive me and help me to reflect You better as Your ambassador. May my life reflect what it means to be saved through Jesus Christ. The mission to make my life count isn't always easy, so I thank You for Your promise to strengthen me, to help me, to uphold me with Your right hand. As Your Spirit lives in me, give me the courage to walk each day by Your Spirit. Remind me that trusting You is always best, even when I don't see it or understand. Thank You for being a God of hope who fills me with joy and peace so that I, too, may blossom in hope. Place people in my path for divine connection, that through me, Your hope and faithfulness can be seen. Thank You for being so faithful and teaching me the importance of being steadfast and courageous. Help me stay encouraged, knowing that living for You is always worth it.

In Jesus's name I pray. Amen.

Based on: 2 Corinthians 5:20; Isaiah 41:10; Galatians 5:25; Romans 15:13; 2 Chronicles 15:7

The Present Rescue Mission

+

Vindicate the weak and fatherless;
Do justice to the afflicted and destitute.
Rescue the weak and needy;
Save them from the hand of the wicked.
Psalm 82:3–4

From beginning to end, the message of the Bible is one of rescue. God the Father sent His only Son to rescue us from sin and give eternal life in heaven with Him to everyone who believes. But the stories of rescue began long before Jesus walked the earth. From the very moment Adam and Eve chose to go their own way instead of obeying God, the ultimate rescue plan was set in motion.

In its most basic definition, *rescue* means "to free or deliver from confinement, danger, or difficulty."[13] The calling to rescue others, to share hope and good news with them, is not optional. And the opportunity will not last forever. One day the clock will run out, Jesus will come back, and God will make all things new.

Until then and only in His power, we are called to defend the weak and the powerless. Stand up for the bullied. Advocate for those who have special needs. Now is the time to pray and to ask God to put a mission on your heart.

What could you do now to join in God's rescue mission? If nothing comes to mind, ask Him to show you an opportunity. Talk to a trusted adult in your life about what this might look like.

Choose Now

✝

This is the day which the LORD has made.
Psalm 118:24

We are not promised tomorrow. We are not guaranteed next week. We do, however, have this moment, the time we are given when we wake up each day. God gives us today as a gift. He wants us to use today to grow, to love others well, to help someone, and to chase dreams He's put on our hearts.

Today is our day to live without fear of the unknown, to live without being chained by failures or what-ifs. No matter what today holds, we can choose to say yes to the opportunities of this moment.

The Latin saying meaning "Seize the day" comes from a longer sentence in the Roman poet Horace's work *Odes*: "Carpe diem quam minimum credula postero." It is translated as, "Pluck the day, trusting as little as possible in the next one."[14] Make the most of your life by choosing now to make the most of your day.

What would it look like to seize today for the Lord?

This Is a Race. Run.

+

Let's run with endurance
the race that is set before us.
Hebrews 12:1

Usain Bolt is arguably the fastest person in the world. He won his first-ever Olympic gold medal at the 2008 Beijing Games when he clocked a world record time of 9.69 seconds during the 100-meter race. The following year at the world championships in Germany, Bolt broke his own world record, clocking in at 9.58 seconds.

Most of us are not competing in track-and-field world championships. We all *are*, however, participating in the race of life. The author of Hebrews encouraged us to run that race with endurance. Not to jog. Not to take a thousand breaks. Not to do the bare minimum to just get by. Endurance means a steady fight, a commitment to carry on even when you don't feel like it.

God has called you to live with purpose. It's your chance to take the platform (big or small) that you've been given and make it count.

What distractions are slowing you down on your faith journey? List two things you can do to avoid getting sidetracked by them.

Nonstop Urgency

+

You are also to be like people who are waiting for
their master when he returns from the wedding feast,
so that they may immediately open the door for him
when he comes and knocks.
Luke 12:36

I'll never forget watching the Broadway show *Hamilton*, Lin-Manuel
Miranda's unique retelling of the story of Alexander Hamilton.
I enjoyed the show so much that I saw it two more times. The third
time I watched it, I was struck by the song "Non-Stop." The song
captures Hamilton's stubbornness and persistence. When the actor
playing Hamilton sang the line "Like you're running out of time," I
was blown away at the urgency with which this real-life person had
lived his life.

I want my journey of faith to be characterized by that nonstop
urgency too.

We have a mission on this earth to share God's love with others.
The world is filled with hurting people who need to hear the good
news. We must live our lives with a sense of urgency in how we
love, give to, and serve others. One day Jesus will return and time
will run out. Are you living with this sense of urgency?

**What is one thing you can do, starting now,
to be prepared for when your Master returns?**

For Such a Time

✝

If you keep silent at this time, liberation and rescue
will arise for the Jews from another place, and you and
your father's house will perish. And who knows whether
you have not attained royalty for such a time as this?
Esther 4:14

Scholars believe Esther was a teenager when she became the queen of the most powerful man in Persia, King Ahasuerus. He didn't know it at the time, but she was Jewish. Then there came a time when Esther couldn't hide her ethnicity anymore. The king had ordered the mass murder of all Jewish people. This nightmare became an opportunity for Esther. She had to make a choice and act fast.

Forced to reveal her background, Esther asked the king to spare the lives of the Jewish people. The reveal could have cost Esther her own life, but the call she knew she had been given was greater. With complete dependence on God, Esther risked the king's anger. And God came through. He softened the king's heart and saved the Jewish nation from annihilation.

There will be times you have to make the choice to do the right thing. God has prepared you for such a time as this.

Is there a decision you must make that might cost you popularity or likes? What will you decide to do?

Get Sent

+

The harvest is plentiful, but the laborers are few.
Luke 10:2

I'll never forget the time I met an inmate on suicide watch at a men's prison when I visited along with my two friends. The prisoner had been found guilty of murder. The warden mentioned that the prisoner was willing to try anything to take his own life.

The second I peered through the small plexiglass window on the padded cell door, the man's eyes met mine. He burst into tears, crumpling to the floor like a rag doll. Once he composed himself, we talked for a bit. He told me that five minutes earlier, he had prayed to God for the first time in a long time. He'd prayed, "I have no hope. If You're real, show me something! If not, I'm going to do anything I can to kill myself!" Five minutes later, there we were. I led the man to the Lord that day. God had a special plan for this young man: an appointment to meet with Jesus.

Lives are at stake. People need Jesus. Ask God to use you to help others move out of the darkness and into the light.

**Who do you know that needs the light of Jesus?
Tell them about Him today!**

Time to Work

✝

We must carry out the works of Him who sent Me
as long as it is day; night is coming, when no one can work.
John 9:4

In John 9, Jesus and His disciples were walking when they passed a man who had been blind since birth. The disciples asked Jesus why the man was blind. He told them it was so the work of God could be displayed in him (see verse 3) and shared with them the words written in today's scripture. Then Jesus healed the man by applying an odd muddy (and rather gross) concoction of His own spit and dirt from the ground.

Can you feel the sense of urgency in Jesus's words? Six months later, He would die a painful death on a cross. He knew His time on earth was limited, so His mantra was "Let's get to work!" He left us an example to follow in every area of life. In this Scripture, Jesus tells us to work now for the kingdom.

It's not always about our timelines and which pleasures or plans we can squeeze in; it's about what we can do for the kingdom of God with the time we are given.

Do you feel a sense of urgency when you interact with people who don't know Jesus? Why or why not?

Do the Hard Thing

✛

Daniel made up his mind that he would not defile himself
with the king's choice food . . . ; so he sought permission . . .
that he might not defile himself.
Daniel 1:8

Daniel and his friends were taken captive to serve in Babylon under King Nebuchadnezzar. They were forced to take new names and indoctrinated in the new culture. But wanting to honor God, they chose to remain close to their convictions.

As a slave, Daniel was allotted food that God had called unclean. Unwilling to go against what he believed, he made a request that could have cost him his life: to eat a modified meal. He chose to take a stand, not knowing where it would lead him.

As a result of Daniel's desire to follow the Lord's commands, God gifted Daniel with wisdom and skill like no one else had. The hard choice may cost you, but God is gracious to those who honor Him.

Like Daniel, do the hard thing, even if it's unpopular. Taking the easy path only leads to mediocrity and monotony, and the plans of God do not settle for those.

Are you willing to do the hard thing? How can you ask God for help in making difficult choices?

Know the Cost

✝

*Which one of you, when he wants to build a tower,
does not first sit down and calculate the cost, to see if
he has enough to complete it?*
Luke 14:28

Peter loved Jesus. That's why, when Jesus told His disciples of His impending death at the Last Supper, Peter made a passionate claim: "Lord, I am ready to go with You both to prison and to death!" (Luke 22:33). His bold claim came in an emotional moment, but when he was put to the test shortly after, he denied Christ three times for fear of what would happen to him.

Are we making passionate claims without considering the cost? Many of us as Christians would be quick to say we are willing to lay down our lives and follow Jesus, but like Peter on the night before the Crucifixion, do we chicken out when trials come?

If we desire to follow Christ and live out the purpose He has for us, it will cost us our comfort. Are you willing to pay the price?

**In what way might God be asking you to
get out of your comfort zone today?**

Boldness and the Holy Spirit

+

When they had prayed, the place where they had gathered
together was shaken, and they were all filled with the Holy
Spirit and began to speak the word of God with boldness.
Acts 4:31

The point of our mission-possible lives is spelled out in the
Great Commission at the end of Matthew 28. It is to spread the
gospel to the ends of the earth and make disciples. Does it sound
like an impossible task to you? Maybe you even wonder what it actually
means.

In Acts 2, Peter delivered a sermon, and three thousand people
got baptized after listening to his message (see verse 41). This was
the same guy who, only weeks before, denied Jesus three times after
declaring his passion for Him. The difference between these two
instances was that Peter was now filled with the Holy Spirit.

Choosing to get uncomfortable is hard on our own. However,
one of the things the Holy Spirit does is give us the boldness to
share what we need to share and do what we need to do. Apart
from Him, we may be daunted. But with the Spirit dwelling inside
us, we can do far more than we ever imagined we could.

**How would you describe the
Holy Spirit's influence in your life?**

Complacency

+

Demonstrate the same diligence . . . so that you will not
be sluggish, but imitators of those who through faith
and endurance inherit the promises.
Hebrews 6:11–12

Have you ever reached the summit, the end of a challenge, only to discover there's still more to climb? Or after you've taken the final exam and think you'll never have to study again, you're reminded there's more to do next semester?

Sometimes this happens on our faith walk. For a time, we are consistent in spending time with God. Life is fairly stress-free, and before we know it, we start to slack off. We become comfortable with life as it is and feel no need to depend on God as we once did. We begin to let our spiritual guard down.

Don't give in to comfort, even when life is going easy. Continue to grow closer to God in the good times so that you can endure and inherit the promises.

**What can you do to keep from letting down
your guard spiritually?**

The Safe Option

✝

There is a way which seems right to a person,
But its end is the way of death.
Proverbs 16:25

When Abram originally received the call from God to move to a new place, his nephew Lot was with him (see Genesis 12). The land they shared suddenly felt a little too small for both of them. Abram suggested that instead of fighting they separate for the good of their relationship and told Lot to choose where he wanted to live (see Genesis 13).

Lot chose the way that seemed right to him. He took the good farming land, near Sodom and Gomorrah. In the end, his choice led to destruction, not to the good life he imagined it would.

Choosing to play it safe instead of following God can actually lead to danger, as it did for Lot. When we fail to seek God and choose based on our own ideas about what is best, we often fail. Because Abram trusted God, he eventually saw His promises fulfilled. When you make the decision to trust God in the unknown, you can also witness His will coming to life.

Are you making decisions based on what you can see, or are you relying on God to lead you? Why?

Train for the Prize

✛

Do you not know that those who run in a race all run, but only
one receives the prize? Run in such a way that you may win.
1 Corinthians 9:24

For a season in my life, the thing I was most passionate about was
sports. I would sometimes wake up in the middle of the night to
train just because I knew no one else was doing it. I knew I was
working toward something bigger, so I wasn't afraid to get uncomfortable. I made it my mission to train for the prize because it was
important to me.

What's important to you?

As Christians, we have the greatest prize waiting for us at the
end of our race: eternal life with Jesus. We receive the gift of salvation through faith, but faith is not a onetime event. We need to
practice our faith continually. This means trusting God even when
it makes no sense to us and going where He leads even if we're not
exactly sure where that is.

Like I trained for sports all the time, we must also practice our
faith constantly. This means trusting God and getting uncomfortable in small moments, not just in the big ones.

**In what small ways can you practice
your faith in God?**

Risk Looking Like a Fool

+

By faith Noah, being warned by God about things
not yet seen, in reverence prepared an ark for the
salvation of his household.
Hebrews 11:7

God had a strange command for Noah. In a world filled with people so corrupt that God regretted ever creating them (see Genesis 6:6), Noah stood out for his righteousness and faithfulness. So when God told him to make a giant boat in the middle of nowhere, possibly miles away from water, with enough room for his family and two of every animal because there was a big flood coming, Noah did it.

Everyone thought the man was nuts. But Noah's faith in God's word kept him doing something that made no sense, even if there were days he must have felt like a fool doing it.

Do you feel as though God is instructing you to do something that makes no sense to you? Something that will invite judgment and criticism? God moves when we take risks and trust Him, even if it makes us look foolish.

Are you concerned about what others may think of you if you step out in faith? Why or why not?

Greater Than the Giants

✝

The land through which we have gone to spy out is a land
that devours its inhabitants; and all the people whom we saw
in it are people of great stature. . . . We were like grasshoppers.
Numbers 13:32–33

Guest devo by Dr. Rick Gardner
Relationship to TTF: physician at Tebow CURE Hospital
in Bulawayo, Zimbabwe

Recently, I was driving at dawn to the CURE Hospital in Kenya and passed an old truck carrying vegetables with the following statement beautifully painted on the bumper: "God is greater than the giants you face." I remember wishing I could ask the driver about his personal reasons for painting this biblical truth on his truck.

The Israelites were seeking to enter the Promised Land after forty years in the wilderness. They sent some spies ahead who returned with disturbing news: The land was occupied by giants, a seemingly insurmountable problem. The spies had a natural fear of the unknown and felt they had to tackle the challenges ahead in their own strength. Joshua, their leader, told them not to be afraid because God was with them. Joshua had God-sized vision and knew they would be stronger for having defeated the giants—that God would be glorified. As in our lives, it was only when the Israelites were moving forward that they found the giants; when they turned back, there were none to be found.

When you face giants, remember you serve an amazing and faithful God who is with you every step of the way.

**Find a prayer partner who is willing to do spiritual
battle with you and, through the power of God,
help you overcome your giants!**

Simple Love

✝

The one who does not love does not know God,
because God is love.
1 John 4:8

Guest devo by Maureen
Relationship to TTF: Night to Shine volunteer and
mom of special-needs daughter

One of the many blessings of having a special-needs daughter was the gift she had to love others without any conditions. Our sweet Brittaney did not recognize anyone's differences; she loved *everyone*. I remember being at a doctor's visit one day and a sweet, precious girl was sitting in the waiting room with us. The little girl had been born with severe physical facial abnormalities and was very shy. Her mom told us later that she was uncomfortable talking to people. Brittaney just started showing this little girl the teddy bear she always carried around with her. Before you knew it, this girl was smiling and laughing with her.

Brittaney's simple love showed our whole family that it did not take a lot of material things to love people. She taught us to embrace our moments together and just enjoy what we have—and laugh a lot!

In 1 John 4, the author wrote that if we are children of the One whose very nature is love, then we will be like Him. Practice simple love. Learn to love in a way that when your presence is not there, the joy and love you experience in God remains with others.

How do you experience simple love with people
by showing compassion?

God Is for You

✝

What then shall we say to these things?
If God is for us, who is against us?
Romans 8:31

Despite what is happening in your life right now, God is still right there by your side working. Whether you see it or not, He has amazing plans for your life. What is happening in your life may be hard, heartbreaking, and painful, but it doesn't change your worth in God's eyes. It doesn't change the truth about how He feels about you. Isn't that encouraging?

Don't let mistakes or failure keep you from experiencing His presence. God is so much more than we could ever imagine. He has no limits. He offers us more love, kindness, grace, and forgiveness than we could conceive of on our own. When you feel abandoned by those closest to you or trapped by a reality you can't understand, there's Someone who has promised to never leave nor forsake you.

God isn't impressed with a list of our good deeds. He doesn't wait to love us until we've gotten every area of our lives under submission. He just wants you. He wants your heart. You are enough!

When you experience failure, how can you remember to run toward God instead of bolting in the opposite direction?

A Prayer for Awareness

✝

Lord, sometimes I live as if I have all the time in the world. I forget there's a community out there, a school, a neighborhood that needs You. Forgive me when I miss the mark. Open my eyes and my heart to see just how much the world needs You. Help me to see each day as a gift that You have created, each filled with opportunity, hope, and purpose—even the days that are hard and uncomfortable. Remind me that there is purpose to this life and that You have called me to run, not jog, stroll, or pause every few hundred feet and grab a snack. You have created me with intention and the capability to do the things that You have called me to do. I can know what they are and do them, and even more, because of You.

In Jesus's name I pray. Amen.

Based on: Luke 10:2; John 9:4; Psalm 118:24; 1 Corinthians 9:24; Ephesians 3:20

It's Not a Popularity Contest

✝

We have this treasure in earthen containers,
so that the extraordinary greatness of the power will be
of God and not from ourselves.
2 Corinthians 4:7

We live in a high-pressure society where reputation is often determined by popularity or follows and likes. But here's some news: You don't need everyone to like you. You don't need to fight for anyone's attention or people-please your way to a higher status.

It can feel good to be liked or have all eyes on us, but that's not our mission. We are called to be kingdom-minded people, pushing the attention away from ourselves and placing it on the King.

A mission-possible life is one that is continually focused on Jesus. We are earthen containers, potted clay formed by design. A flowerpot is not admired for its own beauty but created for a unique purpose: to hold a beautiful arrangement of flowers. Like that flowerpot, we are simply jars designed to hold a precious treasure. The ultimate glory belongs to God, not us.

Life is not a popularity contest. Remember the humble strength of the clay pot, which holds a beauty that is not its own. All glory goes back to God.

**Do you do what you do because you desire approval
from people or from God?**

Brace Yourself

✛

Be on guard. Stand firm in the faith.
Be courageous. Be strong.
1 Corinthians 16:13, NLT

It is your posture, not your strength, that enables you to withstand attack. It doesn't matter how much muscle you have built. If you are off balance, anyone can knock you over. But if you are braced, even if you don't have the most muscle mass, it is harder for an enemy to topple you.

To be braced means that you are prepared for whatever you encounter.

How do you find the right posture from which you can face life's challenges and obstacles? When you meditate on God's Word consistently and pray without ceasing, you will stand tall in God's strength. From that stance of quiet trust, you will withstand the offenses that come your way.

Don't rely on your own strength. Brace yourself in God and remain steadfast in the unshakable foundation of His truth.

**How can you prepare your heart to remain steadfast
as you live mission possible?**

You Won't Always Be Liked (and That's Okay)

✝

If the world hates you,
you know that it has hated Me before it hated you.
John 15:18

We live in an age where people live to be liked. It's normal to want to belong and be accepted. But at what cost?

Like most people, I've aimed to get praise. I am a natural people pleaser, and this has been a hard lesson for me to learn. After a big win or an inspirational talk, I would get likes or high fives. But it didn't take long for me to realize that likes are fleeting.

There is more to a mission-possible life than being liked. As Winston Churchill said, "You have enemies? Good. That means you've stood up for something, sometime in your life." When your conviction is stronger than your desire to be liked, it may ruffle some feathers.

God is going to call you to do some unpopular things, and you won't be liked by everyone. Jesus wasn't liked by everyone, and neither were His disciples. Will we, like the first followers of Jesus, decide that our mission is worth risking our popularity?

Would you rather be liked or do something that makes your life count? Why?

Set Your Mind

+

Set your minds on the things that are above,
not on the things that are on earth.
Colossians 3:2

When you feel the sting of criticism, it's natural to want to obsess over it. One negative comment can affect my entire mood, which can affect my day and even my relationships with loved ones. But I know one thing: I have a choice. So do you.

You don't have to let your mind be consumed with the negativity you hear. You don't have to play that one comment about your outfit or performance over and over in your mind. You can set your thoughts on something else, something that reminds you that you are more than someone's opinion of you.

Science supports this choice to reset your mind. As I've mentioned before, your brain is constantly changing based on your experiences and your habits. By consistently setting your mind one way, such as focusing on the goodness of God instead of the negativity in the world, you can literally transform your brain.

Focus on the things above you and the truths that will last forever.

**When someone says something bad about you,
what can you think about instead?**

Respect over Likes

✝

Only conduct yourselves in a manner
worthy of the gospel of Christ.
Philippians 1:27

Instead of looking to others for validation and acceptance, what if we aimed to earn their respect?

To earn a like or high five, all you need to do is give people something they can identify with—something that will spark a memory, cause a laugh, or tug at a heartstring. Earning respect is much harder. You need to work for it. You need to show integrity, hustle, grind, tenacity, and grit and make the right choices. Not needing the approval of others is the mark of confidence.

Respect is so much deeper than a like, than just saying what people want to hear. What matters is your willingness to keep showing up and doing the right thing, regardless of what others are saying. This is what people will notice when they look at you.

You earn respect not by blending in but by standing out. Stand up for what you believe in, even when it's unpopular. Keep going in faith, even if there's no one with you. Make your mission to please God, not man.

**How can you display integrity today that might
earn someone's respect tomorrow?**

Overcoming Opposition

✝

The thief comes only to steal and kill and destroy;
I came so that they would have life, and have it abundantly.
John 10:10

We have an enemy, Satan, who seeks to steal, kill, and destroy. He doesn't want you living a mission-possible life, doing what God has called you to do. He wants you to obsess over negative thoughts. While it is nice to believe that if you are following the path that God has put before you, you will never encounter opposition, that's not what the Bible teaches. You *will* face resistance. You *will* deal with criticism. There is no escaping it, but here's great news: You can overcome it.

You don't have to give in to the negativity that bombards you. Remember that Jesus, the Good Shepherd, who guides you with wisdom and gentleness, wants to give you an abundant life. He is bigger than what you face. He offers freedom and life, and they're yours for the taking. If you are feeling overwhelmed with negativity in your life, go to Jesus and receive the life He has to offer.

**When you are hit by a blast of criticism,
how can you overcome it?**

He Cares

+

Cast all your anxiety on Him,
because He cares about you.
1 Peter 5:7

People are people. This world isn't perfect, and you will feel the pain of rejection and be hurt by the relationships in your life. Sorry. The fact is, humans at some point will let you down, on purpose or unintentionally. So what do you do when that happens?

Take it to Jesus. First Peter 5:7 tells us that God *cares* for us. He wants us to tell Him all that we feel.

When fishermen cast their nets, they don't casually slip them into the water. They chuck them into the sea with intention and aim, for an actual purpose. So, when we cast our cares on the Lord, we don't simply tell Him in passing all that bothers us. We thrust our anxiety deliberately into His arms, trusting that He will work with whatever we give Him and that He will care for us in the process. When you face ridicule, throw your cares on Jesus. He's got you!

Do you believe that Jesus cares for you?
If so, would you cast your cares to Him today?
Write down your prayer to Him in the space below.

One Step at a Time

+

The LORD directs the steps of the godly.
He delights in every detail of their lives.
Psalm 37:23, NLT

The average person takes about 7,500 steps a day. If you consider the average life span to be eighty years, once a baby learns to walk, that person will walk about a distance of 216,262,500 steps, or 110,000 miles.[15] That's like as much as almost five times around the earth!

Walking around the planet a handful of times in one lifetime seems like a gargantuan task. It's much easier to process when you break it up, one step at a time. Taking one step at a time in life, however, doesn't seem like enough. We want to know the entire picture, right now. But the Bible is clear: God orders our steps.

One of the best ways to find the correct next step is to do what God has put right in front of you. The following questions help me figure that out:

- *How is God calling me to step out today?*
- *Who has He placed in my path to love right now?*
- *Where has He asked me to make a difference in this moment?*

Instead of worrying about your future, just say yes to putting one foot in front of the other.

**What is something you feel God is
nudging you to do today?**

Let God Be God

✝

Commit your works to the LORD,
And your plans will be established.
Proverbs 16:3

Human beings are created in the image of God, but one thing is certain: We are not God. We may have ideas about what He should do, but ultimately we are not in charge.

There's nothing wrong with dreaming big. I do this all the time! But how God carries out His plans for your life is up to Him. Work on your gifts and talents in a way that challenges you. Don't compare your skill level to anyone else's. When we compare, sometimes it makes us want to give up. I hear this all the time: "If I can't be the best at something, why bother?" "Why bother practicing the piano if I'm never going to make it into Julliard?" "Why bother studying hard if there's no way I'm going to be top of the class?"

It's okay to want to be the best, but it's more important to want to be *your* best. I promise you this: God will use your gifts and abilities in His way and for His plan. Rather than trying to figure out or influence how He will make it happen, focus on *Him*.

**Name and surrender the one dream, goal, or plan
that you have not given over to God.**

You Win!

✝

In all these things we overwhelmingly conquer
through Him who loved us.
Romans 8:37

The *fog of war* is a military term that refers to the confusion and uncertainty people feel in the midst of a battle.[16] The chaos of war can cause important information to become confusing. This fog makes it harder for you to understand what is actually happening. You basically can't see or hear or think straight. This limits your ability to do what you have to do. The fog of war is a legit issue not only in battle but also in the course of our lives.

Here's encouraging news: Even when we don't know what's coming next or we feel stuck, our lives will not end in tragedy. Life ends with triumph. When we know Jesus, we are more than conquerors. At some point, Jesus, the greatest general, steps in and fights for us.

It doesn't mean that walking through our trials is easy. But it means we can look past the fog with the hope that can come only through Jesus.

**Think of the last time you experienced
the fog of war in your life. How does knowing
you are a conqueror in Christ help you prepare
for the next time?**

When You're Stuck, Serve

✝

Do not neglect doing good and sharing,
for with such sacrifices God is pleased.
Hebrews 13:16

When we can't see the full picture of our lives and some of our questions go unanswered, what should we do? Certainly, there is a time to wait on God, but rarely is there a time to do absolutely nothing.

You know what happens when we do nothing? *Nothing!*

Making your life count requires action. Instead of being worried or stuck by the unknown, serve! Love. Give. Be a light where there is darkness. Take the time to listen to someone. Go out of your way to encourage a friend or someone at school you don't usually talk to. Show love where there is none.

The little things we do each day add up to something greater and leave a lasting legacy. Now, that's definitely much better than doing nothing!

Name one thing you can do today to serve someone else—and do it!

Seek to Know God, Not the Details

✝

Oh, the depth of the riches, both of the wisdom and knowledge of God! How unsearchable are His judgments and unfathomable His ways!
Romans 11:33

The unknown is uncomfortable. Among many other things, the pandemic of 2020 (and beyond!) reminded us of that much. How many variants are there? When can school return to "normal"? Most of us struggled with many unanswered questions as Covid-19 transformed life as we knew it.

The Bible offers great wisdom when it tells us to "walk by faith, not by sight" (2 Corinthians 5:7). In fact, the Bible reminds us that everything about God Himself is unknowable. God is so great and so unfathomable, we can't comprehend Him. I'm grateful I can't comprehend all He is. If I could figure Him out, He wouldn't be much of a mystery or that big of a deal! Rather than feel frustrated, we should be encouraged by the fact that there will always be something more to learn about God. Find peace in knowing that His knowledge is greater than ours.

What is one thing you can do today to increase your knowledge of who God is?

The Bible,
Our Guiding Light

+

Your word is a lamp to my feet
And a light to my path.
Psalm 119:105

Each fall, Monarch butterflies gather at the top of the same mountain and migrate together from the United States and Canada to central Mexico. It's a phenomenon that happens year after year. These beautiful creatures don't need GPS devices or apps. How do they do it? They have internal clocks and antenna-based compasses. They also track their route using the sun.

The Bible compares the Word of God to a lamp and a light. The same way we need light to guide our path into a room of darkness, we need God's truth to lead us, especially during times of uncertainty. It's easy to allow fear to keep us stuck, but this is the day to live without fear. It starts by diving into the Bible. Don't just read books about it; read *the* Book!

Do you have a plan to regularly read the Bible?
It not, take a few minutes to create a plan today.

God's Already Written Your Story

✦

He guides me in the paths of righteousness
For the sake of His name.
Psalm 23:3

When I was playing baseball for the Columbia Fireflies, a reporter asked me something like this: "Has there been any moment where you said, 'Man, I should have stuck with baseball when I was young'?"

This question got me fired up. I told him, "I think in life there are times when negativity and doubt and fear creep in. We have a choice in those moments. What are we going to do with those thoughts? How are we going to handle them? And what's the next step?"

Having regret or doubt isn't necessarily bad; it's what you do with those feelings that matters. First, I remind myself of the truth that God works all things for His good (see Romans 8:28). Second, I choose to believe in the goodness of His plan. God wrote my story, and He is always working behind the scenes. I don't have to look back with regret. My job is to stay in the moment and do the best I can at whatever is before me.

How can you be all in with whatever is before you knowing God's already got it figured out?

A Prayer for Trust

✝

There have been many times when I've looked outside of You to find what I need: love, hope, direction. And doing that always leaves me empty and wanting more. Your Word tells me that I am a conqueror through You, not those other things. Forgive me for searching in all the wrong places for what I need, what can be found only in You. When I am afraid of what will or will not happen, strengthen my trust in You. Help me to see the unknown as an opportunity to lean on You. Thank You that whatever comes, You have promised to always be there and that You will not forsake those who seek You. Remind me that You are working all things for good in my life, even the things that hurt and break my heart. I believe that You will somehow bring good from them. I thank You, God, that what You say in Your Word about me is greater than what people think of me. I commit the work of my hands to You. Use it the way You want to.

In Jesus's name. Amen.

Based on: Romans 8:37; Psalm 9:10; 56:3; Romans 8:28; Proverbs 16:3

Don't Stop Learning

✝

A wise person will hear and increase in learning,
And a person of understanding will acquire wise counsel.
Proverbs 1:5

M edicine, engineering, and accounting are just a few careers in which education is required. Learning has great value no matter your job or age! And you don't have to stop learning new things once you get that job or finish school. As new creations in Christ, we are united to the Source of all growth, so we can always continue to improve, grow, and develop.

You can learn while you're in school. You can also read books. Listen to a podcast. Take a course. Ask questions. Be curious. Do self-guided research. Improve your knowledge about whatever is important to you. Commit to staying in a constant space of learning.

You're never too young or too old to learn more!

**Think of (and sign up for) one thing this month
that will teach you something new.**

Get It Done!

✝

The desire of the lazy one puts him to death,
For his hands refuse to work.
Proverbs 21:25

When I was fifteen years old and on a mission trip in the Philippines, I met a boy named Sherwin. Sherwin had a physical disability: His feet were backward and he couldn't walk. The people in his village thought he was cursed. Sherwin moved my heart and inspired me to create the Tim Tebow Foundation, an organization that, through specialized programs and ministries, fights for children and adults who cannot fight for themselves. But making a difference took more than being inspired by Sherwin; it took action. Having an open and tender heart is important. So is wanting to make a difference. But what ties the two together is execution. Jesus didn't just *intend* to die for our sins; He actually did!

Don't settle for good intentions. Take action!

What is one positive thing you have wanted to do but have avoided or put on hold? Do it!

Finish Strong

+

[Look] unto Jesus, the author and finisher of our faith.
Hebrews 12:2, NKJV

In the National Championship Game of the 2009 Bowl Championship Series (BCS), the Florida Gators (the team I was playing on) faced the Oklahoma Sooners. Three minutes into the fourth quarter, we drew even at 14–14 but took the lead ninety seconds later, 17–14. With just over three minutes to go in the game, I threw to David Nelson for a four-yard touchdown. We won 24–14, our second championship title in three years.

Near the end of the game, the coach came up to me and said, "I love you. I'm proud of you. You finished strong." His words struck a chord in that moment. Someone I respected had asked me to do something for him, for the team, and I had come through. But I also realized something deeper in that moment. When I get to the end of my life, I want my Father in heaven to tell me, "Attaboy, Timmy—you finished strong."

Often, progress seems slower than we want. Focus on the goal. Set your eyes on the prize. Stay focused on the Author and Finisher of your faith.

**What would it look like for you to finish strong
in whatever project you are working on right now?**

The Power of Together

✝

I urge you, brothers and sisters, by the name of
our Lord Jesus Christ, that you all agree and that there be
no divisions among you, but that you be made complete in
the same mind and in the same judgment.
1 Corinthians 1:10

Relationships are messy. Whether you're always fighting with your sister or arguing with a bestie, relationships take work. They are also one of the most rewarding parts of being human. God created us to be in relationship. He wired us to connect—to share, give, serve, love, encourage, and learn from others.

Jesus didn't need His disciples to fulfill His mission on earth, yet He let them be an important part of spreading the gospel. They helped push His mission forward. There's a lot to be said about rallying together.

An old saying goes, "A rising tide lifts all boats." When we stand together in unity, fighting for instead of against one another, we make our lives and the lives of those around us count.

**Are you facing a relationship challenge today?
Invite God into your situation and pray for peace,
guidance, and a tender heart.**

Maximize Your Talents

+

Well done, good and faithful servant. You have been
faithful over a little; I will set you over much.
Matthew 25:21, ESV

In Matthew 25:14–30, Jesus tells a parable about a businessman. Before leaving on a trip, this man gave three of his employees some money and a task. To one he gave five talents (a *talent* is a measurement of money—about seventy-five pounds of silver), two to another, and one to another, according to each one's ability. The businessman expected his employees, in his absence, to invest the money and make a profit. When he returned, he was thrilled to see the employee who was given five talents had earned five more and the one who received two talents had earned two more. But the employee who was given one talent buried the money out of fear and returned to his boss just the one talent he was given. The first two employees were praised for their efforts, and the third was scolded.

We are responsible to do the most with whatever God has given us, a little or a lot. Don't hide what God has given you—multiply it!

**When you have done something useful for God
or others, how does it feel?**

Make Yourself Available

✝

I heard the voice of the Lord, saying, "Whom shall I send,
and who will go for Us?" Then I said, "Here am I. Send me!"
Isaiah 6:8

When we think of talent, most of us think of things that attract attention: a musician performing onstage, or an entertaining and engaging speaker. But there are many abilities that don't require a spotlight or a degree from an Ivy League university. One of the greatest abilities we have is our availability.

Isaiah was a prophet when the nation of Israel was in a state of turmoil. At the time, the northern kingdom had been taken captive, and the Assyrians were attacking the southern kingdom. God showed Isaiah a vision of the fall of Israel as well as the restoration of God's people in the future. When Isaiah received this vision, he responded, "Here am I. Send me!" He made himself available even though the future didn't look good.

Be aware of opportunities to serve and love God and others, and take those opportunities! Meet a need you see in your world. Listen. Encourage. Say yes.

How can you make yourself available to God?

Never Forget

✝

Samuel took a stone and placed it between
Mizpah and Shen, and named it Ebenezer, saying,
"So far the LORD has helped us."
1 Samuel 7:12

Nischal Narayanam is the youngest double Guinness World Record holder for memory. When he was twelve, he won his first world record for memorizing 225 random objects within 12.07 minutes.[17] Your memory may not be as awesome as this genius's, but it's an important part of your mission.

One way the ancient Israelites remembered the miracles God had performed was to lay stones as a memorial to Him. In the scripture above, the prophet Samuel placed a stone to remember something incredible that had just happened. In a dramatic fashion, God had defeated the Philistines, who had attacked the Israelites. He had confused the enemy to the point they were unable to do battle. To commemorate the victory and God's faithfulness, Samuel laid down a stone as a memorial.

Don't forget the moments when God works in your life. Always remember that He loved us first and calls us to love others.

List three things God has done for you.

The Honor of Humility

✝

He gives a greater grace. Therefore it says, "God is opposed to
the proud, but gives grace to the humble."
James 4:6

There are moments in life that seem unfair. We believe that we
are doing everything right, but it feels as if the world is working
against us. In those times, we may plead with God to come to our
aid and prove that we are not at fault.

However, although God is for you, what you need to do is get on
His side. We do that by remembering that the world does not revolve around us. Our world should revolve around Jesus.

The verse above is one of the first my parents made me memorize. They taught me the importance of humility. When we humble
ourselves, we're reminded that we don't have the power that God
has. He is God, and we are not. The key is to stop demanding that
He be on our side and instead come alongside Him. This is humility
in action, and this is where we can experience His fullness.

**What area of your life do you need
to humbly submit before God?**

Beyond Personal Gain

✝

No one is to seek his own advantage,
but rather that of his neighbor.
1 Corinthians 10:24

If you've ever watched a horse race, you may have noticed the small leather squares the horses wear near their eyes. These squares, called blinders, serve an important purpose in the event. They prevent the horses from seeing anything around or behind them, thus keeping their attention on what is directly in front of them.

We may not realize it, but many of us go about our day with blinders on. We're so distracted by who's popular this week, who is wearing what, who said what to whom, that we forget there is a hurting world around us. It may be time to take the blinders off. We are called to live for more than ourselves.

While humbling ourselves before God is important, it's also necessary to practice humility with others. When we do that, we think of ourselves less and wonder more, *How can I serve others?* Show others the love of Jesus by making your life less about you and more about your willingness to be His hands and feet.

How can you lay aside your personal interests today in favor of someone else?

Rise Above

+

Everyone who hears these words of Mine, and acts on them,
will be like a wise man who built his house on the rock.
Matthew 7:24

In Matthew 7, two men set out to build a house. The first one gathered his supplies and started building a foundation on which to construct his home. The second man also got everything he needed to build a new place, but he couldn't be bothered to lay a foundation. Eager to finish, the second guy started construction directly on the sand. When a storm came, the first guy's house remained steady. The second guy was left homeless on the beach as the squall flattened his house (see verses 24–27).

There weren't too many differences between the first and second man. Their houses were the same age, they likely used the same building materials, and the storm that hit them was the same one. The only difference was one house had a foundation and the other did not.

When our lives are founded on Jesus and we build upon Him, we are like the man whose house was built on the rock. Storms may come, but they cannot shake us. When Christ is your foundation, you can rise above all circumstances.

**Describe the foundation
on which your life is being built.**

Attitude

+

Each one must do just as he has decided in his heart,
not reluctantly or under compulsion,
for God loves a cheerful giver.
2 Corinthians 9:7

Jesus spotted a poor widow placing two measly coins in the collection box at the temple (see Mark 12:42). Many people had already put their own offerings into the box before that, in amounts far larger than what this woman gave, yet Jesus looked at this woman and praised her. Although the amount wasn't that big to most people, He remarked that she gave more than any of the others (see verse 43). Her offering, as little as it was, was all that she had. As Jesus does, He looked beyond the act itself into the heart behind the act. Attitude matters!

God loves a cheerful giver. He is pleased when we devote our lives to Him out of our love for Him. Worry less about the size of the things you can do for God today and focus more on setting your heart on Him. Give of yourself—not because your parents or your pastor want you to but out of the desire to please the Lord.

**In what ways is God leading you
to give cheerfully today?**

Your Public Self and Private Self

✝

As for you, when you pray, go into your inner room, close
your door, and pray to your Father who is in secret; and your
Father who sees what is done in secret will reward you.
Matthew 6:6

There's something exciting about watching a movie and escaping into a fictional world for a while. For a moment, whatever is happening on-screen is your only reality. The cast is in costume, portraying different characters with various personalities. For a while, you believe that the actors you see really are who they are pretending to be.

The thing is, this often happens off-screen too. We walk around putting on different masks, acting our way through life. Many times, we portray the kind of people we want others to think we are. We post our best moments on social media and take thirty-eight selfies before deciding on the most perfect one.

But having integrity is about being the same person, and doing the right thing, in public and in private. Train yourself to hold fast to your convictions.

Who are you behind closed doors?
Is it the person you want to be?

Give Life, Don't Just Take It

+

Those who refresh others
will themselves be refreshed.
Proverbs 11:25, NLT

Have you ever been around someone who sucks the energy right out of the room? Maybe they can't stop talking about themselves, or every other word out of their mouth is negative. It's hard to hang out with people like this because they seem to drain the oxygen out of the air. I call them life takers.

Then you have the other kind of people, the life givers. Their spirits and speech are full of optimism and hope. They genuinely care, and it shows. They make you want to be a better person. It's truly a joy to be around them.

Every interaction we have with someone is an opportunity to influence that person for the good—to *give* life and not just take it. Jesus is the Author and Giver of life. Today, make a choice to follow His example and be a blessing to someone else. Breathe life into whatever space you set foot in.

**What can you do today to put a smile
on someone's face?**

Jesus Cares for the Broken

✝

The King will reply, "Truly I tell you,
whatever you did for one of the least of these brothers
and sisters of mine, you did for me."
Matthew 25:40, NIV

Guest devo by Jason and Tracy Raitz
Relationship to TTF: adoption-aid recipients

We will never forget standing in Kai's orphanage in Nanjing, China, on his family day. We were there to thank his nannies for taking such wonderful care of him for his first three years of life. The experience of meeting him was overwhelming. For months, we had prayed over pictures of this little boy on the other side of the world, and now we were in the exact spot where those pictures were taken. Kai has phenylketonuria, and because of this, he was in a room with other babies who had special needs.

Kai's nanny looked at us and saw the tears in our eyes. She said, "Only Christians adopt these broken babies." In all our years of following Jesus and being in ministry, we have never felt the presence of God so powerfully than in that room with those "broken babies." But she was right! Jesus was there. Jesus not only cares for the broken, the abused, the abandoned; He desperately loves them and brings hope into their lives because of His sacrifice on the cross. I hope today you will be encouraged to care for and love the broken people in your family, workplace, and neighborhood. When you do, you are representing Jesus and loving broken people.

How can an act of obedience morph into something greater than the act itself?

A Prayer for Understanding

✛

Thank You, Lord, for giving me wisdom and understanding when I ask. Forgive me when I rely on myself instead of on You. Help me to continually learn more and more so that I develop into the person You have created me to be. Remind me that Your ways and thoughts are higher than mine. That is why I can trust You instead of relying on what I think. I know and am grateful that the mission You have planned for me on this earth has a deeper purpose than what I may think it is. Your Word tells me that lack of knowledge is a deadly threat. Help me to become more than just book smart or well versed in worldly knowledge. Give me a hunger and thirst to dive deeper into what it means to follow You, take charge of who I am on the inside, and gain valuable knowledge so I might be a light in darkness. Clothe me with a spirit of wisdom and revelation in the knowledge of who You are and what You have called me to do. I am so grateful.

In Jesus's name I pray. Amen.

Based on: Proverbs 1:5; 1 Corinthians 1:25; Proverbs 2:6; Isaiah 55:8–9; Hosea 4:6; Ephesians 1:17

A Love Like No Other

+

God so loved the world, that He gave His only Son,
so that everyone who believes in Him will not perish,
but have eternal life.
John 3:16

Right before the BCS National Championship Game between Florida and Oklahoma in 2009, I wrote out John 3:16 in eye black under my eyes. Ninety million people would Google the scripture that day. Exactly three years later, during my first NFL playoff game, which was with the Broncos against the Steelers in 2012, the strangest things happened, which I can only attribute to God:

- I threw for 316 yards.
- My yards were per rush were 3.16.
- My yards per completion were 31.6.
- The ratings for the game were 31.6.
- The time of possession was 31:06.

That's more than a coincidence. But this verse means much more to me than a football statistic.

When Jesus was on the cross, dying for our sins, He cried out, "My God, My God, why have You forsaken Me?" (Matthew 27:46). God, His Father, had turned His back on Jesus because of the sin He was carrying. That's terrible, right? But God knew that for that moment, He had to forsake His own Son so He would never have to forsake us. God's biggest love, the love He has for His Son, is the love He offers us, the sinners of the world, forever. Now, that's real love!

What difference does God's love make in your life?

The Nature of God

+

God is love.
1 John 4:16

Have you ever wondered what God looks like? It's easy to mold our vision of Him on our own biases and identities. Maybe we picture God as an idealized version of ourselves. Maybe He has a Midwestern accent or cheeseburgers are His favorite food. Maybe He spends His days in a long flowy robe and sandals.

But the Bible does tell us what God looks like: love. God is love. The Bible doesn't just describe love as an attribute of God but uses love to define His very essence. Love is who God is. It is His nature. Love is what God is and how He shows up.

A mission-possible life is steeped in love, which means choosing the best interests of other people and acting on their behalf. God chose the best for us when He sacrificed His Son to save us from our sins. Each day that we choose the best for others, we see what God Himself looks like, because God is love.

How does God's love nature help you make the right choices?

Our Picture of God on Earth

+

[Jesus] is the radiance of His glory and the exact
representation of His nature, and upholds all things
by the word of His power.
Hebrews 1:3

During Jesus's final meal before His arrest and crucifixion, His friend Philip said, "Lord, show us the Father, and it is enough for us." Jesus replied with these blunt words: "Have I been with you for so long a time, and yet you have not come to know Me, Philip? The one who has seen Me has seen the Father" (John 14:8–9).

Essentially, Philip wanted to know what God is like. He asked for more evidence. And Jesus basically said, "He is like Me, and I am like Him." Philip didn't quite understand this, but Jesus's response sheds light on His true nature. There is no divine difference between the Father and the Son. They are both God, equal in essence and power. Although no one has ever seen God, the reality of His likeness is precisely represented in His Son.

Using your knowledge of Jesus, describe God.

His Loyal Love

+

Give thanks to the LORD, for He is good,
For His faithfulness is everlasting. . . .
Give thanks to the God of heaven,
For His faithfulness is everlasting.
Psalm 136:1, 26

A few months after Demi and I got married, we welcomed three adorable puppies into our home: Paris the dalmatian, Kobe the golden retriever, and Chunk the Bernese mountain dog. Paris is Daddy's little princess. She loves to snuggle and is so sweet (*most* of the time). Kobe is the playful one. He's always jumping into the pool and looking for a nice head scratch. Chunk, well, he's a big ole teddy bear! He is a fun-loving, easygoing, protective fur ball. (Don't tell the others, but I think he's Demi's favorite!) What I love most about our dogs is how loyal they are and how unconditional their love is. No matter how I'm feeling, they want to be around me.

I imagine God's love is similar but to a much greater extent! In Psalm 136, *twenty-six times* the author states how God's "faithfulness is everlasting." Just like this line is repeated throughout the chapter, each and every day God's love is repeated for you and me. It's steadfast and personal.

How have you seen God's loyal love in your life?

He Is Trustworthy

+

Blessed are those who trust in the LORD
and have made the LORD their hope and confidence.
Jeremiah 17:7, NLT

The prophet Jeremiah courageously accepted God's call when he was tasked with delivering unpopular news—warning Israel's southern kingdom of their coming judgment. Because the Israelites had repeatedly broken God's covenant, they would eventually be conquered. But before that happened, Jeremiah experienced the trustworthiness of God in a unique way.

While Jeremiah was in a courtyard prison during a time of war, God told him to buy some land. It was a strange instruction, considering the property was in a war zone. But He knew that even though Israel would be defeated, their land would eventually become their own again. Years later, the dust would settle, and the people of Israel would be free to return home, just as God promised (see Jeremiah 32:42–44).

Jeremiah was literally making an investment in faith. He was choosing to believe that God's promises would come to pass. And they did! After seventy years of exile, the Israelites were welcomed back to their land under Persian rule.

As small or big as this account may seem, nothing is too difficult for God. We can trust Him, because often He knows something we don't.

How can you choose to trust God today?

A Good, Good Father

✛

The LORD is good,
A stronghold in the day of trouble,
And He knows those who take refuge in Him.
Nahum 1:7

I remember reading a story about a teenaged girl who appeared in court for a speeding ticket. She pled guilty, and the judge fined her a hundred dollars. Then he did something amazing. He took off his robe, stepped down from the bench, and paid the girl's fine.

Why would he do that?

Well, the judge was the girl's father. As a righteous judge, he knew that she had messed up and had to pay the consequences. But this judge was also a *good, good father!* Stepping down from his seat of authority, he paid the fine so that his daughter would be free![18]

What a perfect picture of the gospel. God the Father stood up from His throne in heaven, looked down at His children, and saw that a penalty needed to be paid. And out of His love for us, He took the form of a man and gave His life on the cross as a ransom to set us free from sin and death (see 1 Timothy 2:5–6). That's a good, good Father.

How have you seen God's goodness in your life?

Unmatched Holiness

✝

There is no one holy like the LORD,
Indeed, there is no one besides You,
Nor is there any rock like our God.
1 Samuel 2:2

*H*oly is not a word we use every day. (Or if we do use it, we typically don't use it correctly.) *Holy* can be defined as "sacred," "distinct," and "set apart." It implies purity and reverence.[19]

Holiness is the very essence of God's nature and character. He is sacred, sinless, set apart, and profoundly different from anyone or anything. His holiness is not something we can understand, but it should open our eyes to how unholy we are as humans.

In his book *The Journey: Living by Faith in an Uncertain World*, Billy Graham wrote, "Only when we understand the holiness of God will we understand the depth of our sin."[20] God's holiness underlines our need for a Savior. There is nothing we can do to be "good enough" to make ourselves holy. That's why it's only because of God's holiness that we are deemed righteous.

What does the word *holy* mean to you?

Rich in Mercy

✝

God, being rich in mercy, because of His great love
with which He loved us, even when we were dead in our
wrongdoings, made us alive together with Christ
(by grace you have been saved).
Ephesians 2:4–5

In one of my favorite passages in the Bible, God is described as being "rich in mercy." When we were dead in our sin and, by nature, deserving of God's wrath (see Ephesians 2:3), God stepped in. He didn't leave us the way we were. Because of His huge love and compassion, He wanted to help us. He brought us from spiritual death to life—not by anything we have done or will do but completely by His great work and goodwill.

In *The Bible Knowledge Commentary* on Ephesians, Dr. Harold W. Hoehner noted that the Greek word for mercy is *eleos* and means "undeserved kindness."[21] As God has shown us undeserved kindness, we are called to do the same for others.

**We don't earn God's mercy by anything we do.
It's been freely given to us through what Jesus
did on the cross. How can you demonstrate
undeserved kindness in your day today?**

Our Forerunner

+

This hope we have as an anchor of the soul,
a hope both sure and reliable and one which enters within
the veil, where Jesus has entered as a forerunner for us,
having become a high priest forever.
Hebrews 6:19–20

The message of the book of Hebrews is clear: Jesus is superior to all things—to angels, to leaders, to the law, and to the Jewish priesthood. As you probably know, following Him isn't always easy. And we shouldn't expect it to be. But we can endure, be patient, and persevere because Jesus did what we couldn't.

In the verse above, Jesus is described as a *forerunner*. The Greek adjective translated here is *prodromos*. This conjures up an image of someone who runs ahead.[22] In ancient Greco-Roman cultures, *prodromos* was used to describe a spy or soldier sent ahead to gather intel, a scout sent out to explore, or a small boat sent to help larger ships.

Jesus was our forerunner. He is the One who has shown us the way. The One who goes before us. The One who pulls us in. That's the character of our God.

**How have you experienced the Lord
going before you?**

Trusting in the Waiting

+

Wait for the Lord;
Be strong and let your heart take courage;
Yes, wait for the Lord.
Psalm 27:14

Waiting is hard. And it can be annoying. We want what we want, right here and right now. When we talk about waiting on God, it's not that He isn't there already. He is always with us. We don't have to wait for His presence. We can trust that God is still with us, even if He feels far away. We trust that He isn't finished with us or with our lives. We trust that He is still working, even if we don't see it. And as we trust Him, we can wait patiently for what He is going to do in our lives.

When we wait at a bus stop, we know the bus is coming and that it's abiding by its schedule, not our own. If we carry that same confidence to our relationship with God, if we trust that He is going to work in His timing and will reveal Himself in His way, we can wait for Him without getting weary. Trust while you wait.

What makes waiting so hard?

Today's Call

+

Whatever you do in word or deed,
do everything in the name of the Lord Jesus,
giving thanks through Him to God the Father.
Colossians 3:17

When we first meet David in the Bible, he is just a shepherd boy, the youngest of eight brothers. Then suddenly he has a rags-to-riches story and is anointed the next king of Israel, right in the middle of his chores and in front of his family.

But David doesn't go straight from tending sheep to sitting on a throne. There's a moment of celebration, but then David goes back to his chores. Although he'd just been declared the next king, he didn't see shepherding as a task that was beneath him. You may have big dreams and lofty goals in store. That's great! I want to also encourage you to give whatever task is before you your full attention. Yes, even your chores!

If you're volunteering, do it with a smile. If you're in school, study diligently. If you have a ton of extra time on your hands, serve someone. Make a conscious decision to work hard, as for the Lord, in whatever He has called you to do.

Take a moment to reflect in the space below on what your call, big or small, may be today.

Behind the Scenes

✝

It is God who is at work in you, both to desire
and to work for His good pleasure.
Philippians 2:13

After David was anointed king and went back to the sheep, he also helped out his older brothers. One day, while his brothers were on the battlefield, David brought them some sandwiches. When he found them, they, along with the rest of the Israelite army, were hiding in their camp from a giant named Goliath. After David asked them some questions, as little brothers do, he decided that enough was enough. An entire nation was terrified of the giant, but David accepted the challenge of fighting him.

Despite pushback from others, David stood firm in his mission. He knew what he was up against. But he had been there before. In his work as a shepherd, he'd chased off lions and bears and killed them with his bare hands. He was confident that God could help him defeat Goliath too.

Waiting is more than waiting; it's preparing. Even when you don't see it, you can trust that He is working behind the scenes in your life for His purposes.

**How has God worked behind the scenes
in your life in the past?**

A Bunch of Little Calls

+

He said to them, "Go into all the world and
preach the gospel to all creation."
Mark 16:15

Maybe you feel like you don't have a big call like David did. Maybe you're not anointed to be a king or called to preach in front of large crowds. Maybe you feel that God is calling everyone else but misplaced your phone number.

As Christians, we all have the same mission: to spread the gospel and make the name of Jesus known. While you may not be called to the ends of the earth, you are always called to your community, your neighborhood, your school, your family—right where you are. Think about it: If God called everyone to a mission field far away, how would people in your school know about Jesus? To God, there is no small call. Each one is of utmost importance in His eyes.

You might not get this one big phone conversation with God, but maybe He is texting you a lot of little things. Think about what you believe He might be saying. Then respond and say yes.

**What can you do to shine the light of Jesus
and focus on the people around you?**

God Provides in the Waiting

+

He rained down manna upon them to eat,
And gave them food from heaven.
Psalm 78:24

After miraculously leading His people out of slavery in Egypt and through the Red Sea, God brought them straight into a wilderness, where they would wander as nomads for about forty years until they eventually came home to the Promised Land.

It took a lot longer than it should have because of the Israelites' disobedience and forgetfulness of God's faithfulness. But God didn't leave them. While they waited and wandered, He supplied. Where there was nothing for them to eat in the middle of nowhere, no McDonald's or Uber Eats to bring food from the next town over, He provided for them with food straight from heaven, exactly enough for each day.

If you feel like you're waiting on God to tell you when to take the next step, look around you today. How is He providing? What has He given you exactly enough for? He doesn't leave us in the wilderness to fend for ourselves. Even in the waiting, He is faithful and good.

Name one thing that God is providing for you today.

God Is Always Leading

✝

The LORD was going before them in a pillar of cloud by day
to lead them on the way, and in a pillar of fire by night to give
them light, so that they might travel by day and by night.
Exodus 13:21

When we decide to live mission-possible lives and follow where God leads, He doesn't always tell us exactly where He is taking us or when we will get there. The Israelites knew there was a Promised Land awaiting them, but they had no sense of direction as they wandered the wilderness. Without a navigation app, they had to rely on God's guidance.

Even when they weren't sure where they were going, the Israelites knew that God was with them. He was in the cloud at daytime and in the fire at night. If He stayed, they stayed. If He moved, they moved.

A life of faith does not require you to know where God is leading; it requires trusting *that* He is leading. You may not know exactly where you are going, but if you have decided to follow Jesus, you can trust that He is always with you. He will get you where He wants you to be.

Where do you see evidence of God's presence?

The Ultimate Outcome

✝

We ourselves groan within ourselves, waiting eagerly
for our adoption as sons and daughters,
the redemption of our body.
Romans 8:23

Often, what makes us so impatient in the waiting is that we want to know the outcome. We want to know the ending before we're even a quarter of the way through the story. But what do our souls really wait for?

We aren't citizens of this world. Our time here will end. But if we believe in Jesus as Lord and Savior, we know how this story ends. We know the ultimate outcome. At the end, we get to be with Jesus in all His glory.

The apostle Paul goes on to say in Romans 8 that though we do not yet see what our hearts ultimately long for, we can wait with expectation and confidence for the day we will see Jesus. If nothing else is guaranteed in life, our salvation and eternity with Him are. With this perspective, we can wait with patience and joy.

**When your life as a believer on earth ends,
eternity with Jesus begins. How does knowing that
encourage you to be more patient and trust God?**

A Prayer for Restraint

+

Lord, Your Word tells us that You make everything beautiful in its time. While I recognize that truth, sometimes I get impatient, angry, and frustrated. Forgive me, God, and help me not to stay in that space. Help me to be self-controlled and trust You more than I trust myself. Thank You for Your great mercy that is infinite and inexhaustible and for being my Father in heaven, who never changes. Even when I stumble, miss the mark, or make mistakes, I am so grateful that You remain steady and faithful. Teach me to likewise remain steady in my journey with You on earth. When I am tempted to turn to things other than You—like being popular, shopping, clothes, praise, or achievement—remind me it is always, and has always been, You. Thank You for the open invitation to come to and remain in You, for You are forever good.

In Jesus's name I pray. Amen.

Based on: Ecclesiastes 3:11; Psalm 27:14; Ecclesiastes 7:9; Deuteronomy 4:31; Malachi 3:6; 2 Timothy 2:13; Psalm 34:8

Don't Let Your Age Stop You

✛

Let no one look down on your youthfulness,
but rather in speech, conduct, love, faith, and purity,
show yourself an example of those who believe.
1 Timothy 4:12

Guest devo by Victoria Franzen
Relationship to TTF: ministry partner, Impact Baby Rescue,
Johannesburg, South Africa

As a sixteen-year-old missionary born and raised in South Africa, I often felt intimidated trying to figure out my place in the world and how I could make a difference. Having parents who had accomplished so much for the kingdom stirred up fears and insecurity that I wouldn't quite measure up or make a difference of my own.

It has been a journey I've fought and prayed about for a long time. I've come to realize I can't waste my time and days wishing to be older, smarter, or more talented before I can do something important. God can use me; He can use *you*! It isn't dependent on age, experience, or geographical location. What matters is that you have an open heart to whatever God calls you to do and that you are willing to take a step, no matter how big or small.

God has used me to love on abandoned babies at our baby home, tell Bible stories to kids in the impoverished communities, pray for the sick, and show kindness to my two-year-old foster sister. No matter how young you are, God has a plan for you. He sees the bigger picture and has a purpose for all of us, no matter our age.

Have you ever allowed your age to stop you from doing something you felt God calling you to do?

He Was, Is,
and Always Will Be

✝

All things have been created through Him and for Him. He is
before all things, and in Him all things hold together.
Colossians 1:16–17

W hen life throws us curveballs, it's easy to allow doubt to
creep in. *Why me? Why now? Why, God, why?* We doubt ourselves, we doubt God's plan, and often we doubt God. *Why would He
allow something bad to happen?*

Hey, I've doubted. I've asked many a time, *God, where are You? I was
depending on You. I thought You had this!* When you ask questions,
when you doubt, when you wonder if God is going to pull
through—or wonder why He didn't pull through—remember that
doubt is normal. God isn't scared of your questions. Bring them to
Him. But don't let doing that stop you from fighting the good fight
and keeping the faith. It may seem that life is a bundle of chaos and
problems and questions, but God was, is, and will always be. You
can count on Him.

**Do you have an area of doubt in your life right now?
Bring your questions to God and ask Him
to help you keep trusting.**

Only God

✚

Jesus said, "With people it is impossible, but not with God;
for all things are possible with God."
Mark 10:27

In 1986, a certain missionary in the Philippines and his wife began to pray for a baby they hoped to have, and a while later, she became pregnant. They were so excited.

When the couple saw the doctor, however, their excitement deflated. The doctor believed the baby wasn't in fact a baby but a tumor. A bit later, more news: The tumor was in fact a baby, but the baby wasn't healthy, and should the mother continue with the pregnancy, it could cost her life. The mother chose to trust in God and keep the baby. Her entire pregnancy was rough, filled with one medical problem after another. But miraculously, the mother gave birth to a perfectly healthy boy. And she, too, survived.

That day, I got to meet my mom. That's right. That "tumor" was me. I'm so grateful she gave me a chance at life. God has the power to accomplish what we cannot. Choose to trust Him when where you're standing seems impossible.

**Name an impossible dream or prayer that
you are choosing to trust God for.**

The God Who Opens Doors

✝

I have set before you an open door,
and no one can shut it; for you have a little strength,
have kept My word, and have not denied My name.
Revelation 3:8, NKJV

Guest devo by Ockert Potgieter
Relationship to TTF: Night to Shine host, Reni, Ukraine

I remember that evening so clearly. It was the night before my wife and I had to fly out to Ukraine to work on the mission field. We had been struggling for months to get the necessary documents from Ukraine to obtain visas. We ran out of time. Our enemies in Ukraine had bribed the secret service, and the official told us clearly when we called that afternoon, "You will never get this document!"

However, the Lord reminded us of His promise that this is where He wanted us to go. A few phone calls later, we were given what we needed. Problem solved!

One of the assurances you and I have when we follow Jesus is that He will open doors before us that seem impossible to open—doors of opportunity to bring His kingdom, to testify, to pray, to build relationships. He opens doors to countries, job opportunities, hearts. All fling wide open when they are where Jesus is leading us, no matter what circumstances seem to be. And when a door closes, because we trust Him, we are at rest because we know He closed the door and that no matter how hard we try, it will not be opened. Isn't it wonderful to follow Him and trust Him? Even when we have little strength, if we keep believing Him, He will finish what He started!

**Ask an adult in your life about a time
God opened or closed a door for them.**

The Gift of Trust

+

He who supplies seed to the sower and bread for food
will supply and multiply your seed for sowing and increase
the harvest of your righteousness.
2 Corinthians 9:10

During a famine in Israel, the prophet Elijah knocked on the door of a widow's house and said he was hungry. The widow didn't have much left. In fact, she said, "I've only got enough ingredients to make bread for my son and me; we plan to eat it, then die" (see 1 Kings 17:12).

Elijah told her it wasn't a problem and to go ahead and make bread for him first, then for her and her son. And if she did that, she'd never have to worry about running out of food. Even in a famine, God would always provide for her and her son. The woman obeyed. Likely, she believed and trusted God. The Bible tells us that "she and . . . her household ate for many days" (verse 15).

Sometimes God will ask us to do or say things that we may not understand the reason for. But that's just Him asking us to trust that He'll make something possible when we think it's not.

What miracles can God do with
your gift of obedience?

Death Is Never the End

✝

All creation is waiting eagerly for that future day when
God will reveal who his children really are. Against its will,
all creation was subjected to God's curse. But with eager hope,
the creation looks forward to the day when it will join God's
children in glorious freedom from death and decay.
Romans 8:19–21, NLT

The Bible tells another story about the widow from yesterday's devotion. Sometime after the miracle, her son got sick and died. Talk about a sick joke! Why would God do that?

While one day we will join all the saints, past and present, in heaven, free of death and decay, tears and pain, for now we remain on earth. And as we breathe through the hard things, we are invited into opportunities to trust in God.

For the widow, it was a bleak moment. For God, it was a chance to show off.

Elijah threw himself over the dead boy and began to pray. As the desperate and faith-charged words surged from the prophet's lips, the boy's lungs started to rise and fall. And in that moment, death did not have the final word.

For believers, death never does.

**How does knowing that God has prepared
a place for you in heaven encourage you
during tough times?**

Your Power or God's?

✝

With people this is impossible,
but with God all things are possible.
Matthew 19:26

After crossing the Jordan River on dry ground and witnessing the walls of Jericho fall, Joshua knew that God was with the Israelites. When it came to the battle of Ai, though, Joshua took matters into his own hands. He sent out a couple of spies and relied on their advice for creating a battle plan, which ended in great loss. Suddenly the Israelites were terrified. Joshua, in despair, turned to God. After repenting for the nation, Joshua received a new battle plan from God. When he obeyed God's voice, his army was again led to victory. (See Joshua 7–8.)

Sometimes you may try to move forward in your own strength and realize that you can't, in spite of how simple the situation seemed. Even if you have seen God move in your life before, it's important to remember that your ability to overcome did not come from you but from Him alone.

Living a mission-possible life is not about the humanly possible but the God-possible. Don't rely on your own power. Continually go to God and seek Him for direction in all things.

**Are you relying on your own power or
God's power for your next move?**

Eating Solids

✢

Solid food is for the mature,
who because of practice have their senses trained
to distinguish between good and evil.
Hebrews 5:14

Growth is a part of life. We're born as infants, helpless and unable to fend for ourselves. Eventually, we become toddlers learning to explore, then children with questions, until we finally emerge into adulthood, when we are more self-sufficient than ever.

But too many Christians are content to be babies in their faith. Although the best and biggest decision we can make in our lives is to say yes to Jesus, we can still grow from that place. We can do more than sip milk whenever we want a spiritual snack. Our faith needs to grow.

The only way to grow is to feed our souls. To become mature Christians, we need to eat solid foods. Don't just read the verse of the day; study the Bible with your family or a group of friends. Don't just pray only before dinner; pray throughout your day at school. Without these nourishing meals, we are bound to stop growing in faith and get stuck in our walks with Christ. We were created for more. Hunger for more so you can grow in ways you never imagined possible.

What can you "eat" today to make sure you are getting the spiritual food your soul needs?

Bread of Life

+

Jesus said to them, "I am the bread of life;
the one who comes to Me will not be hungry, and the
one who believes in Me will never be thirsty."
John 6:35

What do you want most in life? Where do you invest the majority of your time and energy? We all crave something. It may be fame, fortune, love, or acceptance. Deep down, we desire to be known, seen, and heard, and we make it our goal to obtain the things we want, hoping they can fulfill us.

At the root of all our wants is the desire for peace and rest. But Jesus remarked multiple times that only in Him would we find peace.

Jesus called Himself the Bread of Life. He knows our hunger and tells us that He is what we long for. He is more than salvation for our souls. He's more than a teacher. He is daily nourishment for us, the only One who can satisfy our hunger.

Next time you are feeling unfilled in life, recognize your soul's desire for Jesus and turn to Him. Spend time with Him and let Him be the fuel that keeps you going.

**Is your soul malnourished? How can you make
space for the Bread of Life today?**

Blessed Hunger

+

Blessed are those who hunger and thirst
for righteousness, for they will be satisfied.
Matthew 5:6

Those who know me know that I am a big fan of healthy living. Working out regularly and eating the right things that fuel my body are important to me. The building blocks of healthy nutrition include eating whole foods and minimizing the consumption of refined sugars. Getting in your greens and going for a bike ride every day are great habits that will help you stay strong and healthy. And stay away from the processed junk food that will just make you tired and give you brain fog.

Spiritually speaking, though, it is dangerous to curb our appetites for the things of God. Just like with our natural bodies, the less we consume, the less we want to consume. In the same way, the less we fill ourselves with the things of God, the less hungry we will be for them. Jesus said that spiritual hunger is a good thing. He called those who hunger for God's righteousness blessed. The more we hunger for God, the more He will fill us.

How can you increase your spiritual appetite today?

Wonder

+

Your light must shine before people in such a way
that they may see your good works, and glorify
your Father who is in heaven.
Matthew 5:16

How often do you take time to think about the wonders of God—from remembering His faithfulness to prayers He's answered to the way we feel loved by Him when others may have abandoned us?

Sometimes you can be struck by the wonder of God when you sit outside and admire the falling leaves, a bubbling brook, or a star-filled sky. Carve out time in your day to meditate on how powerful, magnificent, creative, and loving He is. Do this often and let your wonder in Him grow.

As your wonder increases, live the type of life with Jesus that will cause others to be curious about the God who is at work in your life. Shine God's light by declaring the things that He has done for you. Do this in such a way that your wonder is contagious.

**How can your life remind others of
God's faithfulness?**

Wisdom

✝

If any of you lacks wisdom, let him ask of God,
who gives to all generously and without reproach,
and it will be given to him.
James 1:5

God appeared to King Solomon and offered him anything. Solomon asked for one thing: Knowing he had big shoes to fill as a king and grateful for the blessing of his role, he asked God to grant him wisdom. Pleased with his request, God gave wisdom to Solomon.

Solomon's desire for wisdom was coupled with his desire to carry out his role. He did not ask God to do his job for him; he asked God to equip him with wisdom so he could do it well. There will be times in which you will need to make certain choices, and only God-given wisdom is going to help steer you in the right direction.

The good news is that wisdom isn't difficult to find. All we have to do is ask God for it. He will not do our job for us, but when we ask Him, He will generously give us what is required for us to make the next choice.

**Where do you need God's wisdom in
your life today? Ask Him for it.**

Treasure Hunt

✛

The Kingdom of Heaven is like a treasure
that a man discovered hidden in a field.
Matthew 13:44, NLT

What would you do if someone handed you a treasure map, like the kind you see in old storybooks, with an X that marks the spot? Would you hold on to it for a little while, then toss it in the trash? Or would you drop everything to go search for the gold, dreaming of all that you would be able to do with the fortune when you found it? I'm sure most of us would go on the treasure hunt. We would be fools to know that something of that worth exists and not search for it.

You can have something infinitely more valuable than a buried chest of gold. The kingdom of heaven itself is a treasure, and we have access to it, no treasure map required. Salvation and eternal life with Jesus are worth more than anything of value you could ever hope to find. Treat your relationship with Him like a treasure. Seek Him daily; you will always find Him.

**How is the kingdom of heaven better than
what you can find on earth?**

A Prayer for Greater Faith

✝

Father, though I know You call me to live by faith and not by sight, I'll admit, it's hard! Forgive me when I fail to trust in You. I believe in You, in Your power, in Your love, in Your holiness, in Your goodness. And in the moments when my faith slips, help me overcome that unbelief. Help me to remain anchored in You despite what I see or don't see. Give me a growing confidence that makes me believe I can do whatever is before me because You arm me with strength. Thank You for the power and the wisdom You graciously give me. I know that it is greater than the wisdom of humans because it comes from the Holy Spirit. Create within me an insatiable hunger for Your Word because it's in Your truth that I will always be satisfied.

In Jesus's name I pray. Amen.

Based on: 2 Corinthians 5:7; Luke 17:5; Mark 9:24; Philippians 4:13; 1 Corinthians 2:4–5; Deuteronomy 8:2–3; Matthew 5:6

Sacrifice Is Inevitable

+

No servant can serve two masters; for either he will hate
the one and love the other, or he will be devoted to one and
despise the other. You cannot serve God and wealth.
Luke 16:13

Most people understand that if you want to achieve greatness, you will have to give up other things in life, like laziness and playing video games for hours and hours. There's too much work to do to get caught up in those kinds of things.

But there's another side to sacrifice. You may decide that you want to spend your days scrolling on your phone or catching up on YouTube videos, which means you won't have time to do other things. Choosing to play video games instead of studying means you sacrifice doing well on your exam. When you choose mediocrity, you sacrifice greatness.

Sacrifice is inevitable. There is a cost to every choice you make. You cannot serve two masters. Either way you choose to go, you will be sacrificing something. Make sure that what you gain is worth more than what you give up.

**What sacrifice have you made that has helped
you grow spiritually?**

Living Sacrifice

✝

I urge you, brothers and sisters, by the mercies of God,
to present your bodies as a living and holy sacrifice,
acceptable to God, which is your spiritual service of worship.
Romans 12:1

In the Old Testament, sacrifices were a big part of the way the Israelites worshipped God. There were sacrifices for atonement, some for praise, some as apology, and some for thanksgiving. The ancient Israelites were given detailed lists of sacrifices they could offer God, depending on the occasion.

On the cross, Jesus became our living sacrifice once and for all. His blood covered all our sins, making other sacrifices obsolete. He was crucified and died a sinner's death but was raised again to life on the third day. Now, just as Jesus is alive, we are also to present ourselves as living sacrifices to God.

To be living sacrifices for God means we follow Him even when it's hard. Instead of the mantra that society tells us—to "do you"—we obey God and trust His plans for our lives.

**What does it mean for you to be a
living sacrifice today?**

Count It All as Loss

+

I count all things to be loss in view of
the surpassing value of knowing Christ Jesus my Lord,
for whom I have suffered the loss of all things, and count them
mere rubbish, so that I may gain Christ.
Philippians 3:8

I remember walking into the Dallas Cowboys complex one day when I was scheduled to speak at the Omni Hotel. The facility blew me away. The more I walked around, though, the more I started to miss football. The more memories that I had, the more frustrated I got with God. I wished in the moment that He'd had different plans for my life, ones that gave me everything I wanted.

I wonder if you've ever felt the same in your life—wondering why something you hoped would happen didn't. Even when we trust God, sometimes the future will look different than we expected. We may lose out on things we hope for, but these losses pale in comparison to what we gain: Jesus Christ.

Ultimately, when we desire to follow Jesus, we trust His leading and we obey. And though losing something we wanted may sting for a while, our gain supersedes the pain.

What do you need to count as a loss today?

Delayed Gratification

✝

Esau . . . sold his own birthright for a single meal.
Hebrews 12:16

In a well-known social experiment, a group of kindergartners were each given a marshmallow. They were told that if they did not eat the marshmallow, they would be given an extra one. Then they were left alone for a few minutes. During the waiting period, some children squirmed and toyed with their snack, while some waited patiently. Others didn't miss a beat and ate the marshmallow as soon as the coast was clear. More was given to the ones who didn't eat the marshmallow but not to the kids who gobbled it up.[23]

Choosing to live a faith-based life means being willing to give up something now for something better later. It takes understanding the reason for your sacrifice, as well as the power of the Holy Spirit, to say no now for a yes later.

In the Bible, a man named Esau traded his birthright for a cup of lentil stew. I doubt he thought the trade was worth it once his belly was full. God has so much more in store for you than you have for yourself. Before you give in to your craving, consider the cost.

What helps you be willing to lay down your desires for today and trust God to fulfill them tomorrow?

Obedience Is Always Best

✝

Samuel said, "Does the LORD have as much delight
in burnt offerings and sacrifices
As in obeying the voice of the LORD?
Behold, to obey is better than a sacrifice,
And to pay attention is better than the fat of rams."
1 Samuel 15:22

God was specific in His commands to Saul, Israel's first king. Through the prophet Samuel, God had instructed Saul to go into the city of Amalek and destroy everything. So Saul went to Amalek and destroyed *nearly* everything. He kept the king alive as a prisoner and kept some of the enemy's best stuff. There is no such thing as partial obedience. We either obey, or we do not. And in Saul's case, he did not.

God was displeased by Saul's action. And through Samuel, God made clear His disappointment at Saul's decision and declared His regret at making him king (see 1 Samuel 15:11). Ouch.

Be obedient in what God is asking of you. If you refuse and do things your way, planning to make it up to Him, you'll fail. Obedience is a form of sacrifice. If you know God is telling you to do something, do it all the way.

**What step of obedience do you need to take
that you have been avoiding?**

Handing Over Authority

✝

Whoever wants to save his life will lose it; but whoever
loses his life for My sake will find it.
Matthew 16:25

Remember the story of the widow who had only enough flour and oil for one last meal for her and her son (see 1 Kings 17:8–16)? She chose to trust God and prepared food for the prophet. God blessed her because of her willingness and faith.

Is God asking you to sacrifice something? Is it your video-game time? A certain friendship? Something you've been watching or doing? As good as it may be, seem, or feel, it will not sustain you. It may be scary to let it go, but when we make the decision to sacrifice the little bit we have, we find that God has more than enough to offer.

When you sacrifice for the Lord, you get Jesus, who is infinitely more than you could have ever tried to earn on your own.

What is God asking you to sacrifice?
Take a leap of faith and trust Him and obey.

By Our Love

+

By this all people will know that you are My disciples:
if you have love for one another.
John 13:35

They will know we are Christians by our *love*. Not by our hashtags. Not by our T-shirts. Not by the highlights in our Bibles or how many verses we post on social media. The one thing Jesus will use to let the world know that we follow Him is our love for others.

When Jesus spoke the above words from John 13, He was sitting with His disciples at their last Passover meal. In this final pep talk, He gave them a new commandment: "Love one another; just as I have loved you" (verse 34).

That is how Jesus told us to love others: the same way He loves us.

Has He given you mercy when you deserved punishment? Has He invited you to come as you are?

We are supposed to love others with that same kind of love. It is hard because it feels so unnatural to us as imperfect humans. Ask Jesus today to help you love others as He loves them.

How can you practice the love of Jesus today?

Can't Pick and Choose

+

My brothers and sisters, do not hold your faith in our glorious
Lord Jesus Christ with an attitude of personal favoritism.
James 2:1

The world is filled with many different people with many different backgrounds, views, and experiences—and they need Jesus too. We must be intentional about loving others, regardless of our differences. We can play favorites with friends and decide who we do or don't want to vacation with, but we shouldn't play favorites with whom we are called to love.

Jesus modeled what it was like to love people who are not like us. While He walked this earth, He visited the home of tax collectors (see Matthew 9:10–13; Luke 19:1–10), who were seen as traitors and thieves. He started a conversation with a Samaritan woman (see John 4:1–42) despite centuries of civil unrest between their cultures. He even washed the feet of His own betrayer (see John 13:1–17).

We can't play favorites. Jesus commanded us to love others, with no loopholes allowed. Trust that the people God has put in your life are there for a reason. Look continually to Him for grace to love them as He loves.

**How can you show love today to a person
who is hard to love?**

Don't Get Discouraged

+

Let's not become discouraged in doing good,
for in due time we will reap, if we do not become weary.
Galatians 6:9

From the time it is planted, an acorn takes four to six weeks to germinate. During this time, the seed in the acorn begins to sprout. First, roots begin to grow. Eventually, a shoot makes its way to the surface. Only then is there something to show for all that has been happening.

Jesus talks about planting seeds—about people hearing the Word of God and the way it may take root in their lives. Sometimes the seeds land in fertile soil. Other times, they don't even have the chance to sprout. As you plant seeds and share the love of Jesus with others, sometimes you might see an amazing heart change right away. At other times, though, you might feel like the message goes in one ear and out the other.

In those moments, remember that you would never plant an acorn and expect an oak tree to immediately spring up. Trust that the seeds you plant will land in fertile soil and that, in time, they will grow.

**How can you encourage a friend who is
discouraged today?**

What's in a Name?

+

Jesus said to her, "Mary!" She turned and said to Him
in Hebrew, "Rabboni!" (which means, Teacher).
John 20:16

On the Sunday after Jesus's crucifixion, just before the sun came
up, Mary went to the tomb where His body had been buried.
To her dismay, the tomb was empty. Jesus's body was gone. Mary
ran out to a gardener in the yard and asked if he knew anything.
Looking at her, the man said one word.

"Mary!"

Instantly, Mary came undone. This person knew her name. She
knew who this person was. He was no gardener. He was Jesus.

Jesus could have said anything to Mary that morning to let her
know who He was. Instead, He just spoke her name.

Never underestimate the power of such a simple act. Something
as small as learning someone's name can remind them of their
value in this world. Obviously, when we say someone's name, it
doesn't have quite the same impact as when Jesus does it. But we
can still show someone we care enough about them to know them
by name.

**Jesus called Mary by name and reminded her
that He knew who she was. How can you give that
same care and attention to someone today?**

Be Intentional

+

Little children, let's not love with word or with tongue,
but in deed and truth.
1 John 3:18

When you are living a mission-possible life and want the world to know about the hope you have and can offer others, you may be surprised to find that those who need it aren't exactly lining up at your door to ask you about it.

There is no doubt that darkness exists in this world and that people feel hopeless, but when you are living in the dark, you have no idea that you are in darkness until you can see the light. We can't sit back while we wait for people who need the gospel to come to us. We need to seek out the lost.

This means acting as if every moment with a stranger is an opportunity from God to share the message of hope. Whether it's the new kid at school or an old friend who doesn't even know you're a Christian, take ten minutes to invest in the people around you. Ask questions. Get to know them. Listen. You may be surprised by what God can do with your obedience and your willingness to get to know others.

**What could being intentional with others
look like in your life today?**

Share the Good News

+

The Spirit of the Lord God is upon me,
Because the Lord anointed me
To bring good news to the humble;
He has sent me to bind up the brokenhearted,
To proclaim release to captives
And freedom to prisoners.
Isaiah 61:1

This Isaiah verse gives us a good depiction of the strategic gospel and how to share it:

- "Bring good news to the humble." In this context, the Hebrew word for humble means poor and needy. The more you talk to people with intention, the easier it is to know when a person is in need. Share with them what you know.
- "Bind up the brokenhearted." If you see someone going through a hard time, sharing the gospel in that moment might mean holding their hand through it and sticking around when everyone else leaves.
- "Proclaim release to captives and freedom to prisoners." Where people are bound up, they need to know that freedom is an option. Be the person to remind them that they don't have to stay stuck. Tell others about Jesus and the freedom that is found in living with Him.

**How has the gospel transformed you,
and how can you share that with others?**

Let Your Life Be Your Message

✝

You are the light of the world.
A city set on a hill cannot be hidden.
Matthew 5:14

Sharing the gospel is not about saying the right words or having the perfect conversation. It's not about developing tricks to get people to invite Jesus into their lives. When we talk of a strategic gospel, we do not mean there is a formula to follow but instead a principle. At the root of it, your life is the message. People can sense fakeness from a mile away. If you really want others to know the saving power and grace of Jesus Christ, your love needs to be genuine. In other words, practice what you preach.

Jesus said in Matthew 5:14 that we "are the light of the world." We shine His light in and around us simply by following Him. The glory of God will be evident through our actions alone, especially through the way we behave with others.

What do you want your life message to say?

A Prayer to Imitate Jesus

✝

Lord, what a great example You left for us when You walked this earth. You gave it all up to come down from heaven to love, teach, guide, serve, and ultimately give Your life for us in the greatest form of sacrifice in history. Like a sheep led to the slaughter, in humility and obedience, You came to die, and live again, so we can live with You in eternity. Help me see the sacrifice You made for humankind not just in Your death but through Your resurrection. When I get discouraged from doing what You have called me to do, strengthen my spirit. Remind me that You look for a spirit of obedience, that You are looking for Your children to surrender to You rather than make grand sacrifices that make us look good in front of others. Help me to think of others more than myself—not in a boastful way but because it is Your model of mission-possible living. Finally, when the pressure is on and the darkness around me builds, remind me that within me is the Light of the world. Strengthen my heart, mind, body, and spirit to overwhelm the darkness with light.

In Jesus's name I pray. Amen.

Based on: Philippians 2:5–8; Isaiah 53:7; Galatians 6:9; 1 Samuel 15:22; Romans 12:3, 21; John 8:12

Hold Fast

+

Let's hold firmly to the confession of our hope without
wavering, for He who promised is faithful.
Hebrews 10:23

Guest devo by Rich and Michelle Franzen
Relationship to TTF: ministry partners, Impact Baby Rescue,
Johannesburg, South Africa

In the world we live today, the daily pain, suffering, and death we
see around us seems to be increasing. Living nearly eighteen years
in Africa, we have definitely seen our share of hardship. Poor education,
abuse, and poverty denote the impoverished communities
in which we work. Most often the victims of these atrocities are
babies, children, women, and the marginalized.

There are days it is just too much. We need something to grab
hold of to keep us secure, focused, and operating in the Lord's
strength.

The author of Hebrews was clear in saying, "Hold firmly to the
confession of our hope without wavering." A different Bible version
says it this way: "Let us seize and hold tightly the confession of
our hope without wavering, for He who promised is reliable and
trustworthy and faithful to His word" (AMP).

As we grab hold of the truth of God's Word, it helps us steady
our wobbly legs and stand on His promise to be reliable, trustworthy,
and faithful. In turn, it helps us bring hope to the hopeless by
giving them something to grab hold of as well: Jesus!

**What are you grabbing hold of in the midst of
the storm? How are you helping others
grab hold of the truth?**

Let God Use Your Pain

+

Rejoice to the extent that you partake of Christ's sufferings,
that when His glory is revealed, you may also
be glad with exceeding joy.
1 Peter 4:13, NKJV

Ethan Hallmark was nine years old when he was diagnosed with stage IV cancer. Four years later, he entered heaven.

Over a third of his life was spent facing endless rounds of high-dose chemo, stem-cell transplants, multiple surgeries, more than one hundred days of radiation, and travel for trial after trial. He suffered a lot, but that was only part of his fight. Ethan wanted people to know the truth that the glory to come, the glory found in the priceless gift of Jesus Christ, was far greater than any amount of suffering endured in this temporary world.

While Ethan waited to beat cancer, he used the darkness to bring others closer to the light of Christ. Through his life and death, Ethan affected so many people, even bringing countless men and women, as well as boys and girls, to make the decision to trust in or rededicate their lives to Jesus.

Pain is painful. But God will use even the hardest and most desolate parts of our lives for a purpose far greater than we can imagine—but *only* if we let Him.

**What is the worst pain you've ever experienced?
What helped you endure that pain?**

Stay in the Heat

✝

He knows the way I take;
When He has put me to the test, I will come out as gold.
Job 23:10

People have been refining gold for centuries. In Bible times, they did it with high-temperature flame. Gold was first mined from the earth, cleaned of dirt and debris, then crushed. The next step involved removing the dross, which is the gold's waste product and has no value. The clean gold was then placed in a container called a crucible over a hot fire. Dross formed on the surface and the refiner skimmed it off, leaving behind only pure gold. This process was repeated over and over. I've read that some refiners considered their work finished when they could see a reflection of themselves in the gold.

The Bible uses the image of "refining by fire" to describe a process that is uncomfortable but brings forth a purer image of Jesus Christ in our lives. When it gets too "hot," we want to run away. But when we stay and trust the process—yes, even in the pain—we will become more and more like Jesus.

What have you learned through a "refining by fire" experience? Ask an older person in your life about one of their experiences.

On Whom Is Your Hope Set?

+

We despaired even of life. . . .
We would not trust in ourselves, but in God who raises
the dead, who rescued us from so great a danger of death,
and will rescue us, He on whom we have set our hope.
2 Corinthians 1:8–10

In his second letter to the church at Corinth, Paul was open about his troubles. He wanted the people he served to know that he and the ones who served alongside him had been wrecked beyond their expectation. The Passion Translation puts the above verses like this: "All of the hardships we passed through crushed us. . . . It felt like we had a death sentence written upon our hearts."

This is intense! Scholars have different theories as to what was happening with Paul. Whatever was going on, it was a rough time. Yet it was also an opportunity for him to set his hope on God. I can't tell you the purpose for your or a loved one's pain, but I can say that it reminds us to trust less in ourselves and more in the God on whom Scripture promises we can set our hope.

Take a few minutes to think about the present situation in your life, or that of a loved one, that is causing pain. Then pray. Ask the Lord to give you His eyes and His heart for that situation.

The Message in Your Story

✛

Let's consider how to encourage one another
in love and good deeds.
Hebrews 10:24

My dad is one of my greatest heroes. For my entire life I've watched him choose a path that usually bears struggle, pain, and hardship—but a path that's worth all of it. Over the years, Dad has told us kids a ton of stories from the mission field. One story that stuck with me was a time when right before he was due to preach, some armed men rushed him and said, "If you preach, we're going to kill you." Dad responded with courage. He walked up to the podium and told those men and the others who came to listen to him how much God loved them.

When Dad got Parkinson's disease, his doctors told him to stop traveling and take it easy. He didn't. He told me he was going to keep sharing the gospel the same way he had been doing for the past several decades. I want to follow in Dad's footsteps.

The Bible is full of stories that can inspire, encourage, and challenge us. Don't view your struggles as pointless. Ask God to help you reframe them into opportunities He will use to share hope with others.

**What do you hope people can gain when
they hear about your story?**

It Is Well

✝

Behold, I extend peace to her like a river.
Isaiah 66:12

We won't always know or even understand the purpose of our pain until we get to heaven, but because the God we serve has gone through unimaginable physical and emotional torment, we are assured He cares for us amid heartbreak, as a nursing mother tends to her baby.

Horatio Spafford was a lawyer who lived in Chicago with his wife and five kids. He went through incredible hardship, including the loss of his four-year-old son. A religious man, Horatio kept his faith and did the best he could to make the most of his life. Two years later, while his wife and four daughters were away on the first leg of their family trip, Horatio received a telegram from his wife. The ship that she and her daughters had been sailing on had been in a terrible accident, and the four girls had drowned. A few days later, Horatio was on a boat to meet his wife. At the same spot where his children had died, he wrote the hymn we know today as "It Is Well with My Soul." As wrecked as he was from the pain of loss, Horatio was able to live in the strength of the only One who could make his soul well.

How has God strengthened you in a hard situation?

The Bigger Picture

✝

"I know the plans I have for you," declares the LORD,
"plans to prosper you and not to harm you,
plans to give you a hope and a future."
Jeremiah 29:11, NIV

Guest devo by Ansley Jones
Relationship to TTF: W15H Recipient

Two weeks after my fourteenth birthday, I was diagnosed with a very aggressive blood cancer, and two months after my sixteenth birthday, I relapsed. Altogether, I have spent nearly a year of my life in a children's hospital, endured extensive amounts of chemotherapy, received a bone marrow transplant, and suffered from almost every possible side effect. Throughout my cancer journey, this verse solidified my faith in God and gave me comfort in knowing that He has good things planned for my future.

On February 15, 2021, I celebrated my fifth anniversary of being cancer-free. I'm not glad that I got cancer, but because I did and survived what felt like a never-ending uphill battle, I have grown more as a person, and for that I am thankful. God was there when I was at my lowest, and He gave me strength when I needed it most.

This verse reminds us that even when we are suffering or in pain, it is only temporary. The Lord has plans to give us hope and a future. Problems we face may seem insurmountable in the moment, but it is important to take a step back and remember there's a bigger picture at play. God has a purpose for our lives, even though we may not be able to see what it is in the moment.

Think of a time in your life when something did not go as you had planned. How did God show you that He had designed a different path?

The Gift

✝

"My grace is sufficient for you, for power is perfected in weakness." Most gladly, therefore, I will rather boast about my weaknesses, so that the power of Christ may dwell in me.
2 Corinthians 12:9

Guest devo by Rachel Hallmark
Relationship to TTF: mother of W15H recipient Ethan Hallmark

After four years of fighting cancer, my thirteen-year-old son, Ethan, had run out of options. During his palliative care, we took a trip to a Christian camp in Colorado. When the counselor asked each teen what their gift was, Ethan's reply left him speechless: "Cancer is my gift." How could a dying teenager view cancer as something to be used as a gift?

What if creating a life that counts involves unthinkable suffering?

Are you weak and weary today? While your heart aches and tears fall, the very power of Christ rests upon you. In His sustaining grace, you can create a life that shows others there is so much more than this world. His power is evident when others see that nothing—not a terminal illness or any other trial you walk through—can take your eyes off the prize of Christ.

The gift for Ethan was never in his dreadful disease but in the hope of Christ that others saw in him despite his suffering. As those powerful words came out of his mouth, Ethan knew the gift was in using his cancer to glorify God as he pointed others to Christ.

No matter how big or small the trial before you,
how can you use it to glorify God
and lead others to Him?

Give God Your Weakness

✝

My flesh and my heart may fail,
But God is the strength of my heart and my portion forever.
Psalm 73:26

A man I admire is the father of one of my best friends. Though he had a history of trauma, his story is of transformation. Throughout his childhood, this man had multiple stepfathers in and out of his life. All of them were violent. As he grew up, he began to train in martial arts. Fighting became an outlet for his anger. But soon the anger grew into rage and bitterness.

Finally, he met Jesus. Over time, this man learned to surrender his bitterness to God. He realized that committing to trust in Jesus wasn't a partial promise. He had to be all in. Everything had to change. It wasn't a perfect or clean transformation, and it took a lot of inner work, patience, and time to process his trauma. Watching this man love God and let go of his bitterness has had a profound effect on my life. The aftermath of painful experiences may seek to destroy our lives, but we can always depend on a God who will give us strength.

**What bitterness, pain, or anger is
God inviting you to give Him today?**

Great Is God's Faithfulness

✝

The LORD's acts of mercy indeed do not end,
For His compassions do not fail.
They are new every morning;
Great is Your faithfulness.
Lamentations 3:22–23

When Thomas Chisholm wrote the lyrics to the classic hymn "Great Is Thy Faithfulness," he understood what it was like to find God to be faithful even as he suffered greatly on this earth. Chisholm's life was not a worldly success story. Without any formal training, he served as a minister for a year. Then health problems, including the sudden and uncurable loss of his hearing, ended his ministry. But his devotion to God never waned. Through the ups and downs, Chisholm found solace in the Bible. The above passage in Lamentations had a special place in his heart. He used it as the basis for "Great Is Thy Faithfulness," which has since become one of the most popular hymns of all time.

Life is hard, painful, and confusing, but God is good. He can be trusted even when circumstances seem to say otherwise. And His faithfulness—a strength cultivated in our weakness, and new every morning—will never fail.

**Think of some moments when God was faithful
to you even when you felt hopeless.**

The Place of Strength

✝

If I have to boast,
I will boast of what pertains to my weakness.
2 Corinthians 11:30

When we think of sharing our stories, most of us focus on the crowd-pleasing moments. The overcoming. The successes and triumphs. But the moments that made us cringe tend to stay hidden.

The apostle Paul didn't hide certain parts of himself. This was the guy who wrote with honesty, "The good that I want, I do not do, but I practice the very evil that I do not want" (Romans 7:19). That wasn't his pride talking. Paul wasn't the kind of guy to humble-brag. He exposed his weakness to highlight God's strength.

It's hard to share where we fell short, how we messed up, or how our best effort didn't result in a win. When we do share those, it's not because God wants us to broadcast what losers we are. It's not about us. It's about showing how perfect God is—the God that we serve, believe in, and trust in our weakness. Be bold. Don't cower from admitting a truth that could give hope to someone else. Weakness is not the end of the story. It's about a God who shows up and in that exact weakness perfects His strength.

**Where can you find God's strength
in your weakness?**

Greater Than Our Hearts

✝

LORD, You are our Father;
We are the clay, and You our potter;
And all of us are the work of Your hand.
Isaiah 64:8

God is always in the process of molding us, and this process is not easy. Some might say that walking by faith is simple—or that it should be. But most things that are worth doing aren't simple. Sure, it was easy for me to get super pumped and put Bible verses in eye black under my eyes when I was winning championships and scoring touchdowns. It's easy to praise God when you're crushing life and when everyone loves you. But when a giant stands in front of you, what does your faith look like?

A friend of mine likes to say, "God is greater than your heart." When hardships show up—and they will—we must choose faith. Rather than allow our hearts to remain in a state of emergency, discombobulated and overly anxious, we can choose to believe that God is greater than whatever is disrupting our stability. We must choose faith.

We must choose to believe in Him whether or not we feel like it.

**How has God molded you through a difficult time?
Can you say you are better for the experience?**

The Power of Weakness

✝

I delight in weaknesses, in insults, in distresses,
in persecutions, in difficulties, in behalf of Christ;
for when I am weak, then I am strong.
2 Corinthians 12:10

Guest devo by Robyn Clarke
Relationship to TTF: W15H recipient

I've lived with cerebral palsy for twenty-one years. As I've become an adult, I've wrestled with how others see me. When someone notices me across a room, do they see a girl worth knowing, or am I defined by the walker I use to get around?

Not long ago, a thought crossed my mind: What if my physical weaknesses are intentional so that I can witness God's power as He guides me through obstacle after obstacle?

God never makes mistakes. Everything about you—your hobbies, your passions, your dreams—are threads in a larger tapestry, one that He has woven to bring a greater plan to fruition. When you find yourself wondering if God is working through you, find peace in the knowledge that you are His. He has chosen you. One day you'll look back and realize that what you considered your biggest flaw may actually be your greatest asset.

How have you seen God use your weaknesses to make a difference in someone else's life?

We Are Not Crushed

+

We are pressed on every side by troubles, but we are
not crushed. We are perplexed, but not driven to despair.
2 Corinthians 4:8, NLT

**Guest devo by Slone Kays
Relationship to TTF: W15H recipient**

In my short twenty-five years of life, I have suffered and survived more than I could have ever imagined. At the age of fifteen, I had brain surgery, received a brain-and-spinal-cancer diagnosis, and started chemotherapy. As a child, I was resilient and knew I would beat this disease. However, when I relapsed at age twenty-four, I had a more negative mindset. *I'm going to die. This cancer is going to kill me this time* were the words I told myself most days in the beginning. It felt like everything was falling apart all around me.

Soon into my second time having chemotherapy, that "Why me?" mindset changed. I began to think, *Why not me? I can do this!* I fought because I knew God had a plan for me. I knew there was a reason He kept me fighting. I wasn't, and still am not, going to give up this fight as long as I have my God by my side. He has shown me that no matter the situation, I will not be crushed. I will persist.

**Has God put you in a situation recently where
you felt crushed? How can you call upon Him
to help you persist through this season?**

Joyful Suffering

✛

None of these things move me; nor do I count my life
dear to myself, so that I may finish my race with joy,
and the ministry which I received from the Lord Jesus,
to testify to the gospel of the grace of God.
Acts 20:24, NKJV

**Guest devo by Hanna Liv Workman
Relationship to TTF: Joint Venture Ministry,
Tebow Okoa Philippi Campus, Masaka, Uganda**

In our first six months of living in Uganda, we faced a number of challenges. People tried to throw acid on us, kidnap our daughter, poison our water supply, destroy our ministry and reputation, and put us into prison! So many days I wondered what was happening and why!

In the verse prior to the one above, Paul said that the Holy Spirit had assured him that chains and tribulations awaited him on his way to Jerusalem. Yet he was going anyway. Why? Because he counted his life as no value to himself. In plenty and in suffering, preaching God's grace to people was the only thing that mattered, not his own needs, feelings, or well-being.

When we live with an eternal perspective, we find peace in knowing that our lives—our victories and failures, our comfort and suffering—are not about us. Keeping our eyes on heaven helps us remember that life here on earth is short compared to eternity. And what could matter more than something that lasts forever? There is no greater joy or satisfaction than knowing that we are living, celebrating, and suffering with an eternal purpose.

**Think about the last time you felt joy
in a moment of hardship.**

What Are You Talking About?

✝

We proclaim to you what we have seen and heard,
so that you also may have fellowship with us. And our
fellowship is with the Father and with his Son, Jesus Christ.
1 John 1:3, NIV

Guest devo by Mike and Missy Wilson
Relationship to TTF: ministry partners, myLIFEspeaks

When our family first moved to Haiti, we knew that the remainder of our lives would not be easy. But one thing we did (and still do) know is that we would rather be where God has called us than anywhere else. The longer we have lived here in Haiti, the more we know that God's call is not to make Haiti more comfortable. Instead, our call is to tell everyone of the great things we have seen and heard God do in our lives and in Haiti.

We believe God is the only true hope for the world, and because we believe that to our core, we often talk about His goodness, the gospel, and the salvation that only He can bring. If you claim to love Jesus above all else but aren't filled with His fruit or aren't changed by His love, others see you as saying one thing but living another. Your *life* speaks greatly to what your heart is truly about.

Today, choose to shout about the goodness of God with your entire life and not just your words.

Whose story are you telling: yours or God's?

A Prayer for Strength

+

God, do not be far from me today! I am tired and worn out. I've come to the end of all my "trying," and I admit that I can't do it all on my own. I desperately need to be reminded that You, and You alone, are my ultimate source of strength. As my heart and mind grow weary, I am reenergized knowing You are an ever-present help in times of trouble.

Lead me to Your dwelling place, for in my weakness, Your power is perfected. Apart from You, I can do nothing. Your name is a strong tower, a shelter for when I am hurting. You hear my cries. You listen to my prayers. Fill me with courage and an awareness that You are with me wherever I go. May I run, as one pursuing righteousness, into the refuge of Your loving arms. It is there where I find comfort in my pain. Your grace is sufficient, for when I am weak, then I am strong.

In Jesus's name. Amen.

Based on: Psalm 22:19; John 15:5; Psalm 46:1–3; 61:1–4; Proverbs 18:10; Joshua 1:9; 2 Corinthians 12:9–13

The Privilege of Prayer

✝

Let's approach the throne of grace with confidence,
so that we may receive mercy and find grace
for help at the time of our need.
Hebrews 4:16

The Old Testament book of Leviticus records the rules required of the ancient Israelites. Because God is a holy God, it was necessary for them to keep themselves and everything they touched holy and clean. There were also particular instructions for the Levitical priests about how to make sacrifices and how to dress and behave when worshipping God. These rules were a tall order to follow, but it was the only way that they would be guaranteed access to God.

When Jesus gave His life on a cross for our sin, He took the place of all those written laws. Sin had separated us from God, but Jesus's sacrifice restored our relationship with the Father. When Jesus died and rose again, He made a way for us to approach God directly.

Prayer is a privilege. Through it, we can talk directly with God. We can tell Him anything and everything and listen expectantly for His response. As you live a mission-possible life, it's important to stay in touch with God. Do it through prayer.

**Do you view prayer as a privilege
or a chore, and why?**

Constant Access

✤

Pray without ceasing.
1 Thessalonians 5:17

If I were to ask you how often you talked with your best friend, you'd probably tell me something like, "All the time!" That's what our prayer life should be like. Think of it less as something you *have* to do and more as something you *get* to do! It's not for God's benefit but for yours!

This doesn't mean that your prayer life is limited to on-the-go prayers when you're on the way to school or practice or when you need help to pass that test. Just as you make time to hang with your friends, make time to hang with God.

Think how awesome it is to be connected to the Source of life itself! We get to talk to God in the middle of our crazy day, when we're struggling, when we're afraid, and when we're trying to wrap our minds around unexpected news.

If you have a worry, you can bring it to God then and there. If you want to thank Him, you don't have to wait until later that night. Wherever you are, whatever you are doing, you can always talk to Him.

**What prayer do you want to bring
before God right now?**

Hallowed Be Thy Name

✝

Pray, then, in this way:
"Our Father, who is in heaven,
Hallowed be Your name."
Matthew 6:9

When Jesus died to restore our relationship with God, He gave us even more than access to our Father in heaven; He gave us the ability to personally get to know the Creator of the heavens and earth. Prayer is more than just a conversation with God; it is the recognition that He, holy and righteous and mighty, desires to have relationship with us. The same God who placed the moon in the sky wants to know us and be known by us. Wow!

Prayer is about setting our focus back on God. First and foremost, we need to acknowledge all that He is. To pray without ceasing does not mean that we pray flippantly or focus on only ourselves. When we pray, we should come before Him with respect. Out of that reverence, we learn to submit to God, and through our submission, we will see the transformative effects of prayer in our lives.

What can you worship God for today?

Bring It to Him

✝

My God, my God, why have You forsaken me?
Far from my help are the words of my groaning.
My God, I cry out by day, but You do not answer;
And by night, but I have no rest.
Yet You are holy,
You who are enthroned upon the praises of Israel.
Psalm 22:1–3

Have you ever been angry with God or felt hurt at something that happened or something someone said? Do you carry those burdens to God in prayer or keep them to yourself?

If you read through the book of Psalms, you'll find that David often cried out to God in his despair. He didn't hide what he felt from the Lord—he brought it *to* Him. In doing so, David always remained secure in the presence of God. A man after God's own heart, he knew that God could handle his emotions. Because of David's confidence in God, he was also able to trust Him when it was hard.

Some seasons in life are tough, and prayer may feel impossible. But in those seasons, turn to God with your weakness and frustration instead of trying to sort through it yourself. When we present everything to Him in prayer, He gives us peace in return (see Philippians 4:6–7).

When you feel bad, do you tend to run toward God or away from Him? Why?

Powerful and Effective

+

Confess your sins to one another, and pray for one another
so that you may be healed. A prayer of a righteous person,
when it is brought about, can accomplish much.
James 5:16

When Elijah earnestly prayed for a drought on the land of Israel, rain did not fall for three and a half years (see 1 Kings 17:1–7). Then when he prayed that it would rain, it suddenly did (see 18:42–45). James reminds us that Elijah was just as human as we are, but his prayer had tremendous power. Just like Elijah, when we are made right in God's eyes through the blood of Christ, we can pray bold prayers.

The Bible teaches us to confess our sins to one another and pray for one another. It says that when we, as people made righteous through salvation in Christ, pray, our prayer can accomplish much. When we pray, whether for loved ones or ourselves, we can expect God to move because He cares.

**When have you ever seen God move in
great ways through prayer?**

For More Than Ourselves

✝

I urge that requests, prayers, intercession, and
thanksgiving be made in behalf of all people, for kings
and all who are in authority, so that we may lead a tranquil
and quiet life in all godliness and dignity.
1 Timothy 2:1–2

If you were to keep a journal of all your prayers over the past
month, who would you see that you prayed for the most: yourself
or others?

We are called to *intercede* for others, which, according to the dictionary, means "to intervene between parties with a view of reconciling differences; mediate."[24] Prayer is more than just about us.
Through prayer, we can stand in the gap for another person.

We are also called to pray for people who may not know God
personally. The Bible instructs us to pray for our leaders and whoever is in authority. This is true whether we like them or not! Prayer,
in general, is humbling because it reminds us that God is God and
we are not. What better way to stand back and let Him do what He
does best!

**Who might God be asking you to
intercede for today?**

Listen for the Answer

+

I will stand at my guard post
And station myself on the watchtower;
And I will keep watch to see what He will say to me.
Habakkuk 2:1

Prayer is not just a one-way conversation with God. Like Habakkuk, we can make our requests to God and ask Him questions, but we also need to stand still and wait for His response. Too much of the time, we hope that He will chase us with His answer, but just as you wouldn't walk away from someone after asking a question, you don't want to walk away from God before He answers.

God always answers prayer. The answer may not be what we are hoping to hear, but we can be expectant for His voice—not an audible one but a quiet whisper in our hearts. If it feels like God has been silent lately, go back to where you last spoke to Him. Remain there until you hear His response. Talk to God, but also give Him a chance to talk to you in your heart or through His Word.

**How do you give God a chance to speak
to your heart?**

Even on Your Best Days

✝

Moved with compassion, Jesus touched their eyes;
and immediately they regained their sight and followed Him.
Matthew 20:34

In Matthew 20:29–34, Jesus and His disciples were leaving Jericho and heading toward Jerusalem for what would be Jesus's final Passover celebration. I imagine the atmosphere was electric! Large crowds followed them, many of whom probably had seen His miracles.

But on this day, on this road, Jesus was interrupted by a loud cry. Two blind men, overlooked by society, cried out, "Lord, have mercy on us, Son of David!" (verse 30). The crowd tried to hush the men up, but they cried out even more. Jesus stopped and showed *compassion*. He touched their eyes, and immediately they were healed.

What I love about this is the fact that even on one of Jesus's best days—a day He was being celebrated—He still chose to put the best interests of others ahead of His own. Instead of asking, "What can you do for Me?" Jesus asked, "What can I do for you?" Even on our best days, we don't stop living mission possible!

**When times are good and things are going
your way, how can you still choose compassion?**

Are You
Moved Enough to Act?

✛

When Jesus went ashore, He saw a large crowd, and
He felt compassion for them because they were like sheep
without a shepherd; and He began to teach them many things.
Mark 6:34

Have you ever seen something that touched your heart? Or maybe you've heard a story about some injustice or tragedy that made you want to do something to help.

I imagine you have! Well, throughout the Gospels, there's this interesting word that may describe the way you feel at times. It's the Greek verb *splanchnizomai* (splawnk-nitz-oh-my). Say that five times in a row!

Splanchnizomai appears twelve times in the New Testament and is traditionally rendered "moved with compassion" or "felt compassion." It's built on the root word for a person's internal organs (heart, liver, lungs, and so on). Figuratively speaking, it means the center of deep emotions and feelings.[25] So, when the word *compassion* appears in our English translations, it literally means "to be moved from our inside parts."

What I find most interesting is that in every occurrence of the word, when someone was "moved with compassion," they immediately followed up with an action! It's one thing to say you have compassion, but it's another to actually take action.

**When was the last time you were
moved enough to act?**

To Suffer With

+

Do not plead with me to leave you or to turn back
from following you; for where you go, I will go,
and where you sleep, I will sleep.
Ruth 1:16

When a famine hit the land of Judah, Naomi, her husband, and their two sons left Bethlehem and settled in Moab. It was supposed to be a fresh start. However, shortly after arriving, Naomi's husband died. Roughly ten years later, Naomi lost both her sons. The people she loved were gone, and she was then left to fend for herself.

Or so she thought.

Naomi's daughters-in-law, Orpah and Ruth, were still with her. Naomi insisted they leave her and get remarried. But Ruth, a Moabite woman, would not. She was willing to sacrifice her own identity, dreams, and ambitions for the sake of Naomi's best interests.

As I mentioned in a previous devo, our English word *passion* comes from a Latin word meaning "to suffer." Well, we get our English word *compassion* from *passion*. It means "co-suffering" or "to suffer *with*."[26] Ruth was willing to suffer *with* Naomi—in her grief and in her eventual new life back in Bethlehem.

**Has there been a Ruth in your life?
Have you ever been a Ruth for someone else?**

There Is No "Yet"

✝

The LORD is near to all who call on Him,
To all who call on Him in truth.
Psalm 145:18

My friends Jeff and Becky Davidson got married in 1991 and had the rest of their lives planned out. However, they quickly realized they had much less control than they thought.

Their son, Jon Alex, was born with cerebral palsy and autism. He would be unable to walk, talk, or live on his own. Fast-forward to 2009, when Jeff got sick. For years, Jeff was in and out of the hospital. From 2015 through 2017, he was unable to care for himself, and Becky became his caregiver while also remaining Jon Alex's.

In one instance, a social worker from the hospital asked Becky, "Who will take care of Jeff when you return home?"

Becky answered, "I will. We've been married more than twenty-five years, and I'm not going anywhere."

The social worker responded, "Yet." It was a sarcastic way of saying, "Sure, Becky—it's only a matter of time before you leave."

Very directly Becky responded, "There is no yet," and went on to explain how leaving her family was not an option.

Becky's story is a telling example of what it looks like to be all in—to suffer with and have real compassion for people. There was never a time when she was going to stop caring for those she loved.

There is no "yet." Who or what is God asking you to have compassion for?

The Prodigal's Father

✝

He set out and came to his father. But when he was still a long
way off, his father saw him and felt compassion for him,
and ran and embraced him and kissed him.
Luke 15:20

I f you grew up in church, you've probably heard the story of the
prodigal son. As the parable goes, the son asked his father to give
him his inheritance early, left home, and wasted all the money (see
verse 13). When a famine hit, he went to work at a nearby farm
feeding pigs. It didn't take long for him to realize that he'd made a
big mistake. Filled with shame, he went back home. Maybe his dad
would take him back as a hired servant.

And then in verse 20, my favorite part, we're told that while the
son was still a long way off, his father saw him, felt compassion for
him, and ran to him! What I find fascinating is that in the first century, a Middle Eastern man rarely ran. If he were to run, he would
have to pull up his tunic so he would not trip. By doing this, he
would expose his bare legs, which in that culture was shameful for
a man to do. So here we have the most beautiful part: The father
took on shame rather than shame his son.[27]

**How does this story shape your understanding
of God as a Father?**

Fall on Your Knees

✝

Moved with compassion, Jesus reached out with His hand
and touched him, and said to him, "I am willing; be cleansed."
Mark 1:41

In Mark 1:39–45, while Jesus was preaching in Galilee, a man with leprosy went up to Him. At the time, that was social suicide!

In the first century, leprosy was considered a curse. Many thought that people with leprosy had it because they'd done something really sinful. It's a skin disease that causes nerve damage, skin bumps, loss of feeling, and body deformations. Given that leprosy was spread by skin-to-skin contact or by coughing and sneezing, those who had it were cast out from society.

So, I imagine that when this man fell to his knees begging Jesus to heal him, whoever was around stepped back or ran away. But not Jesus. With compassion, He moved toward the man. Reaching out His hand, Jesus did what no one thought He would do: He *touched* the leper, making Himself "unclean," and said, "I am willing; be cleansed." And immediately the leprosy left the man!

Jesus is willing to show compassion. We must make the choice to move toward Him and ask Him to do what we cannot.

**When's the last time you fell on your knees
before God? Perhaps today!**

The Science of Compassion

✝

Rejoice with those who rejoice,
and weep with those who weep.
Romans 12:15

According to a Harvard medical study, 56 percent of physicians said they didn't have the time to be empathetic with patients.[28] Let that sink in for a moment.

This study, among others, is noted in a book called *Compassionomics*.[29] The authors have spent the past several years researching the effects that compassion has had on hospital revenue, administration, patient recovery, and the health-care system as a whole. What they've been wanting to know is whether showing compassion *actually* has scientific impact. Here's what they found: It takes only *forty seconds* of genuine care and compassion from an oncologist to see a huge difference in health outcomes and patient care![30] Forty seconds! The more doctors connect and talk to patients, the better the results!

See, showing compassion isn't just talk. It has meaningful impact!

Take forty seconds today and be intentional with someone who is hurting or just needs some love.

A Prayer for Impact

✝

Lord, first and foremost, I am so grateful You have rescued me. I was once dead in my own sin but am now alive in Christ. With a big smile on my face, I humbly say, "Thank You!" I'm now part of Your rescue team, and You've given me a simple mission: to love You and to love people! By the power of Your Spirit, may I go into my home, my school, my team, my community—everywhere—and tell others of the good news of Jesus, for it is only in You that I find joy and hope.

As I go, take away my selfishness so that I may impact as many people as possible. Let this be not for my own glory but for Yours! I pray that as I enter the dark and hard places, Your Light shines bright for all to see. I want my life to truly matter. I do not want to chase after the temporary things anymore. When my feet hit the floor in the morning, I want to make my life count. I want to pursue the things that last forever: You, Your Word, people, and eternal rewards. May my life be defined by these things.

In Jesus's name. Amen.

Based on: Ephesians 2:1–5; Mark 12:30–31; Matthew 28:19–20; Acts 1:8; Matthew 5:16; 1 Corinthians 9:25; 1 John 3:11, 16; 1 Corinthians 9:19, 23

A Lopsided Life

+

Seek first His kingdom and His righteousness, and all
these things will be provided to you.
Matthew 6:33

Finding balance is less about having everything equally spread out in your planner and more about having everything in its proper place. Balance doesn't mean that everything in your life gets the same attention; it means that you have your priorities straight.

It's easy to get overwhelmed by life's demands. Instead of focusing on *our needs,* we are called to look to *the One* who supplies all our needs.

The secret to finding balance is to live a lopsided life, one centered on Jesus only. He takes care of what we need, physically and spiritually. He cares about the small things in our lives so much that He promised to provide us with all the essentials when we seek His kingdom before all else. That means you don't have to strive to attain perfection. You only need to trust Him with all aspects of your life and allow Him total control.

What does it mean to live a lopsided life?

The Glorification of Busy

✝

The Lord answered and said to her, "Martha, Martha,
you are worried and distracted by many things;
but only one thing is necessary."
Luke 10:41–42

Martha was stuck with the cooking after her sister decided to sit with the guests. Between basting the roast and dressing the salad, she sighed loud enough that Mary, in the next room with the guests, would get the message that she clearly needed help.

Finally, Martha had enough. "Jesus," she called to the guest of honor. "Please tell Mary to help me out." Jesus looked down at the sister who was sitting at His feet to learn from Him. Mary had gotten it right.

Often, we forget that God hasn't called us to a life of simply doing. He wants us to serve others with His heart, and the only way to do that is to step aside from our to-do lists and sit with Him and learn from Him for a while.

Don't reduce your mission-possible life to busywork. Spend time with Jesus by reading your Bible and praying. Make Him—not doing—your priority.

**Where in your life do you need to stop *doing*
and start *being* with Jesus?**

Balance for Your Body

✝

Do you not know that your body is a temple of
the Holy Spirit within you, whom you have from God,
and that you are not your own?
1 Corinthians 6:19

As I've mentioned before, I am passionate about physical health. I believe it's important to eat well and give your body the nutrients that it needs not only to survive but also to grow stronger. I want to make the most of every day that God gives me, today and fifty years from now!

Staying healthy isn't for looking good or impressing your friends with how ripped you are. God created our bodies, and if we are Christians, they are temples of the Holy Spirit. A mission-possible life goes only as far as your health allows. Honor God with your body. Get enough sleep, eat well, and exercise. Treat your body well so you can be ready to go wherever He calls you.

How can you better care for your body today?

Balance for Your Soul

+

[Jesus] answered and said, "It is written:
'Man shall not live on bread alone, but on every word
that comes out of the mouth of God.'"
Matthew 4:4

Just as it is important to keep your body healthy, the same goes for your soul. If your spiritual life isn't working to full potential, you won't be able to pursue the mission-possible life that God has called you to live.

Going through life without spending time in the presence of God will make you go hungry. You'll become weak and tired. In order to keep going, you need to nurture your soul regularly. Although we might like to believe that having a quick five-minute devotion time is enough to keep us fed, we need more. We need to read Scripture regularly to nourish ourselves. We need to actively work out what we take in through the Word and allow for times of rest where we pray and allow the Lord to speak to us. Maintain a consistent routine to grow stronger and more ready for whatever the Lord has for you.

How does your spirit need feeding?

Ask People for Help

+

Bear one another's burdens,
and thereby fulfill the law of Christ.
Galatians 6:2

We live in a culture that prides itself on independence. For many people, the goal is to be able to do it all on our own. While it may seem noble to be able to stand on our own two feet, we were not meant to journey through life by ourselves. We need to build relationships and encourage and pray for one another.

The Bible tells us to bear one another's burdens. If the body of Christ is functioning properly, this means that you help others out but also accept assistance from your community. When you feel like you can't handle it all, reach out and ask for help. You'd be surprised how willing people are to pitch in, but they won't unless they know about a need. This requires humility, but in that humility, we allow others to come alongside us and help carry the hard stuff.

**Do you find it difficult to ask others for help,
even when you desperately need it? If so,
how can you change that?**

Ask God for Help

✝

My help comes from the LORD,
Who made heaven and earth.
Psalm 121:2

You know the cliché "God won't give you more than you can handle"? I'm sure Moses would have disagreed. After the Israelites complained about the miraculous manna they were bored of eating, Moses just about lost it. God had given him too much responsibility, and he wanted to quit. Unable to meet the needs of the people God had given him to lead, Moses turned to Him in his frustration. God responded by sending seventy leaders to help Moses.

Are you stressed out by the pressures of school, sports, music, caring for your pet, watching your little sibling, and your other responsibilities? Like Moses, sometimes doing it all feels like too much! Lay your burdens at Jesus's feet. The point of living a mission-possible life is not to take on more than you can handle; it's to live a life dependent on God. When you feel like you are carrying more than you can manage, go to Jesus. Ask Him for help and depend on Him to give it.

**Is there a situation in which you need help?
Ask God for help instead of trying to deal
with it on your own.**

Don't Run on
Only Momentum

+

[Look] only at Jesus, the originator and perfecter of the faith.
Hebrews 12:2

When life seems easy and stress-free, it's tempting to hit pause on seeking God. After forty years of wandering the wilderness, the Israelites were eager to cross the Jordan River into the Promised Land. But before they could, Joshua invited them to stop and consider who had gotten them to that point. They had been led for decades by God's hand to a land flowing with milk and honey, and before they stepped into it, it was important to acknowledge Him. They laid twelve stones as a monument to remember His deliverance and faithfulness. It was also a reminder that He would continue to journey with them.

When living a mission-possible life, acknowledging God is more important than going on momentum. Even when you're excited, instead of getting caught up in running to the next thing, take a beat and look at Jesus, the reason you are here in the first place.

**Are you constantly thinking about the next thing
in your life? How can you put your focus on Jesus?**

Light in the Darkness

+

The light shines in the darkness,
and the darkness has not overcome it.
John 1:5, NIV

Guest devo by Levi Veirs
Relationship to TTF: W15H recipient

Have you ever felt alone or that things are going the exact opposite of the way you want them to go? I have felt like that
many times. In those moments, God continues to show up and remind me that just as He spoke light into existence, His light can
overcome any darkness.

When I was younger, I had a bunch of surgeries that required
intense recovery times. I was in a dark place in my life, and I had a
hard time seeing the good. God knew I was struggling, and He used
those moments to show me just how much He loves me.

If you turn a flashlight on and cup your hand over the top, you
can still see the light through the creases of your fingers. It's as if the
light is fighting to get through. God's love is like that. In those moments when it is difficult to understand why hard things are happening, even though you try to cover it up, God doesn't turn off the
light of His love. He uses every one of those opportunities to pursue you. He will use other people to shine love over you through
their actions and words. He separated night from day to give you
rest and affirm that just as the sun is constant, so is His love for you.

**How have you experienced God's love in
a difficult situation?**

When You Get Rerouted

+

I am obligated both to Greeks and non-Greeks,
both to the wise and the foolish. That is why I am so eager
to preach the gospel also to you who are in Rome.
Romans 1:14–15, NIV

For the longest time, the apostle Paul had his heart set on going to Rome to preach the gospel. He'd prayed about it. And it was clearly in the will of God. I mean, Paul wasn't going there to tour the Colosseum or binge on pasta; he wanted to share the message of Jesus. But despite the apostle's prayers, God had a different plan for him. Eventually, Paul got an opportunity. He was transported to Rome—as a prisoner! He lived under house arrest for two years while his case was being heard. During that time, he wrote four books of the Bible (Ephesians, Philippians, Colossians, and Philemon) and shared the gospel with countless people, including highly ranked officials.

Trust God with your prayers. Understand that your future may look different than your dream, but God will still carry out His plan.

**In your heart of hearts, what do you
dream of accomplishing? Offer up that dream
to God in prayer.**

Take the Risk

✢

One who watches the wind will not sow and one who
looks at the clouds will not harvest.
Ecclesiastes 11:4

Living for Jesus might just be the most incredible privilege we have. However, it's not entirely possible to do it without taking risks. Maybe you're afraid of getting made fun of for sharing the gospel, so you don't, or you're not sure bold prayers are the way to go, so you pray safe ones. Yet the Bible is filled with stories of imperfect humans pursuing mission-possible lives and taking risks in the process. Abraham was one of those people.

When God called Abraham to move and start over somewhere new (see Genesis 12), it wasn't easy but he trusted God and obeyed. When God told him he would become the father of many generations, Abraham trusted God and believed even though he didn't see how it would be possible.

How often do you give God a chance to come through? Don't let something scary keep you from believing that He can do the impossible.

**What's one risk you've been afraid to take?
Tackle it this week.**

It's Not Over

+

The plan of the LORD stands forever,
The plans of His heart from generation to generation.
Psalm 33:11

King Nebuchadnezzar thought that throwing Shadrach, Meshach, and Abednego into the fire would kill them. It didn't. Job's wife tried to convince Job to quit believing and to curse God and die. He didn't. The woman with a bleeding disorder may have gotten discouraged after her tenth year of suffering, but she continued to believe even though she was not healed yet. The stories are different, but the message remains the same: It's not over. (To read these, see Daniel 3:19–27; Job 2:9; and Mark 5:25–34.)

God's love and purposes don't change when hard times come or people disappoint you. You can still make a difference when life gets challenging. When you give your pain and heartbreak over to Him, He will always find a way to use those for good.

The tough times and the trials you go through are real and painful, but it's not over for you. Wherever you are, now can be a beginning. Don't worry about what you've lost or what lies ahead. Watch as God unfolds a plan that has more love, more meaning, and more purpose than you could ever imagine.

**How can you grow your hope that
God's plan for you is good?**

Remember Whom You're Trying to Please

✝

Am I now seeking the favor of people, or of God?
Or am I striving to please people? If I were still trying to
please people, I would not be a bond-servant of Christ.
Galatians 1:10

I love being able to come through for people. What can I say? I'm a people pleaser by nature. I like making people happy, whether that means making wishes come true through my foundation or doing something extra-special for my wife, Demi, just because. But I've learned that if I'm motivated only by making others happy, I'm left with a hollow feeling.

There is nothing wrong with wanting to be the best, with wanting to succeed, or with wanting to win. It's good to have passion and work hard. However, it can become a problem when the desire for praise becomes everything. Why? Because praise doesn't last! After winning the Heisman Trophy in 2007, I was told I was the best in the world. Three years later, I was told I couldn't throw. Though it may make us feel good to please people, it will always make us feel fulfilled to please God.

**How can you tell if you're motivated by
God's approval or by other people?**

The God of Comfort

✝

Just as we share abundantly in the sufferings of Christ, so also
our comfort abounds through Christ.
2 Corinthians 1:5, NIV

Guest devo by Hollen Frazier
Relationship to TTF: ministry partner, AGCI House of Hope

Comfort is something we all crave. Although there is nothing wrong with seeking out comfort, it has a clear enemy: challenge. In my decades of serving vulnerable children and families with All God's Children International (an orphan-care ministry dedicated to showing God's love to every child), there have been many times that we've had to leave what feels comfortable in order to follow God's call and challenge.

As I continue to grow and trust God's plan for my life, I'm learning to change my understanding of comfort. It's not about something being easy; it's about being strengthened by God in the midst of life's challenges. Comfort is not a destination. It is a restrengthening for the road ahead, a mystery captured in that verse (above) to the church at Corinth.

Where do you need some comfort today?

A Personal Love

✛

I am giving you a new commandment,
that you love one another; just as I have loved you,
that you also love one another.
John 13:34

God doesn't just choose to love; love is His nature, His essence, His being. "God is love" (1 John 4:16). Love motivates His every move and inspires His action. It's a reflection of His heart, His character.

Who am I? Who are you? We are the objects of His love. That's a big deal. God loves the world, but He also loves each one of us individually. He is infinite and focuses all His love on you and on me. He can't spread Himself too thin, He cannot exhaust Himself, so every single person on the planet is the object of His love.

In fact, Jesus died for you. You! Did you get that? If you were the only person on this planet, He still would have died for you. That's some powerful stuff!

Knowing we are the object of His love lays the groundwork for our identities. We are adopted into the family of God. We are wanted. We belong.

**List the reasons why you know that
you are personally loved.**

A Prayer of Confession

✛

Father, be gracious and forgive me when I have fallen short. I know I have been made new in Christ, but too often I make the same mistakes and repeat the same bad habits. I admit that

- *I worry when I shouldn't.*
- *I get spiritually lazy and go through the motions.*
- *I miss opportunities to show Your love.*
- *I lack patience and self-control.*

Forgive me, Lord. You're the One who sees everything, and it is against You, and You alone, that I have ultimately done wrong. Wash away my guilt and shame. Give me a fresh start today. Renew my spirit and restore the joy of my salvation!

I am glad You don't despise a humble and broken heart. I come before You willing to do whatever You ask. May Your peace, which surpasses all human understanding, guard my heart and mind today in Christ Jesus!

In His name I pray. Amen.

Based on: Psalm 51; Romans 3:23; Ephesians 4:22; Matthew 6:25; Philippians 4:6–7

Do You Hear the Bombs?

+

The way of a fool is right in his own eyes,
But a person who listens to advice is wise.
Proverbs 12:15

In August 1982, seventy-one-year-old Mother Teresa marched into the thick of a bloody conflict known as the siege of Beirut. As part of the Lebanon War, Israeli planes had bombed the city of Beirut, leaving more than thirty special-needs children trapped in a mental hospital in the middle of the war zone. After becoming aware of the situation, Mother Teresa decided to take action! She was warned by a priest that the risk was too great. But even hearing the bombs blast in the distance, she believed risking her life for Jesus and the children was her responsibility.

The next day, Mother Teresa entered Beirut and somehow negotiated a cease-fire so she could extract and rescue the children. Safe and secure, mission accomplished.[31]

In Proverbs 12, Solomon wrote about how a person who listens to advice is wise—which I believe is true. However, it's important to note that not all advice *is* wise. In the case of Mother Teresa, she had a conviction, but the advice she received was against the mission. Do not let the opinions of others distract you from living mission possible.

Have you ever let the advice of others distract your living on mission?

Comparison Trap

✛

Jesus said to him, "If I want him to remain until I come,
what is that to you? You follow Me!"
John 21:22

We constantly compare ourselves to others. One research study concluded that on average, 12 percent of our thoughts each day are comparison-based.[32] I imagine that number increases with the more time we spend on social media. Even those who were closest to Jesus struggled with comparison.

In John 21, after the Resurrection, Jesus surprised the disciples with breakfast. When they were done eating, Jesus asked Peter three times if he loved Him. Each time, Peter answered yes. Then Jesus proceeded to tell Peter how he would eventually die. When Peter heard this, he looked at his disciple-friend John and wondered, "What about this man?"

Jesus replied, "What is that to you? You follow Me!"

Peter's first thought was comparison. Jesus's response? None of your business!

Jesus doesn't want or ask us to be like anyone else. All He desires is for us to *follow* Him. That means keeping our eyes fixed on who God has called us to be and not on what culture says we should be.

**Do you struggle with comparison? Be reminded
that there is freedom and joy in knowing
that Jesus has a plan just for you!**

Heart Check

+

Where your treasure is, there your heart will be also.
Matthew 6:21

In 2002, Disney released the action-packed intergalactic animated thriller *Treasure Planet*. It tells the story of a fifteen-year-old boy, Jim Hawkins, who stumbles upon a treasure map that supposedly leads to a planet full of gold. Working as a cabin boy aboard a spaceship, Jim follows the map, but his voyage gets interrupted by greedy pirates who are also looking for the same mythical treasure.

Though the film is science-fantasy, there are some lessons to be learned from it. Many of us can be, like the pirates, so locked in and distracted by material things, spending our entire lives pursuing them, that we don't realize they are leading us toward destruction. That is one of the messages Jesus gave in His famous Sermon on the Mount: "Do not store up for yourself treasures on earth, where moth and rust destroy, and where thieves break in and steal. But store up for yourselves treasures in heaven, where neither moth nor rust destroys, and where thieves do not break in or steal" (Matthew 6:19–20).

Every now and then, you need to give yourself a heart check. Be honest and admit what matters most: treasures on earth or treasures in heaven?

Where are your treasures stored?

There Is No Lion

✛

The lazy one says, "There is a lion outside;
I will be killed in the streets!"
Proverbs 22:13

On October 18, 2011, fifty zoo animals were released to roam the streets of Zanesville, Ohio.[33] Imagine coming home from school that day and seeing a four-hundred-pound lion walking on the side of the road.

Well, there wasn't a literal lion in the street when King Solomon wrote Proverbs 22:13. This verse is an illustration about making excuses. He said the reason the "lazy" person will not go outside is that he's afraid of being mauled by a lion. It's a pretty extreme excuse for not doing something.

I wonder how often we say similar things that keep us from carrying out our responsibilities or reaching our goals. Maybe they're not as far-fetched, but I hear excuses like these all the time:

- "I'm not talented or smart enough."
- "I'm too young."
- "It costs too much."

Excuses get you nowhere. This imaginary king of the jungle pales in comparison to how the King of the universe wants to use you.

**God sets us free to run fast toward the things
He's called us to. What excuses stop you
from doing this?**

Entitlement Mentality

✛

This is the way any person is to regard us: as servants of Christ and stewards of the mysteries of God. In this case, moreover, it is required of stewards that one be found trustworthy.
1 Corinthians 4:1–2

One of the greatest distractions in living mission possible is having a "You owe me" attitude. I think we've all been there. But the truth is, we're entitled to—wait for it—*nothing*. In his first letter to Timothy, Paul wrote, "We have brought nothing into the world" (6:7). We have nothing to offer. God created everything and owns everything. And if we are deserving of anything, it's death!

But thanks be to God, for He has given us everything through His Son, Jesus Christ (see Romans 6:23). Not only has He given us the gift of eternal life, but He's also entrusted us to be good stewards of all He has provided.

Creation (the world and everything in it) is God's property, and He has made us stewards, or caretakers, of it. Though it's not ours, we're invited to look after and enjoy it.

Each day on earth is a privilege. How can you avoid an entitlement mentality and steward your blessings today?

"Making It"

+

One who trusts in his riches will fall,
But the righteous will flourish like the green leaf.
Proverbs 11:28

Have you ever said or heard someone say, "When I _____, I'll have made it"?

The blank could be getting a certain number of followers on social media, graduating from an Ivy League school, getting the part in a movie, or making a ton of money. This idea of "making it" essentially means you've reached a level of success that you find completely satisfying. It's arriving at your destination. "Making it" is what many of us live for, but do we have the right definition of what it means?

It's great to have goals, but for believers, the things I listed above are not what it means to "make it." Making it is being in a relationship with Jesus Christ. Making it is denying self. Making it is caring for the lost and broken. Making it is being a generous giver. Making it is showing up to heaven and hearing, "Well done, good and faithful servant" (Matthew 25:21, ESV).

Don't get distracted by how the world defines *making it*. When you stay focused on God's mission for your life, you've made it!

How do you define *making it*?
How might you need to change that definition?

Master the White Belt

✛

The word of the LORD is right,
And all His work is done in faithfulness.
Psalm 33:4

Many martial arts programs have a certain number of belts in varying colors. Each colored belt represents a level of mastery. The more that students study and practice the art, the further they progress.

The white belt signifies a beginner. A white-belt student is someone who desires to learn. In the Christian life, when it comes to reading and studying the Bible, the white belt should be our daily mindset.

Some of my biggest faith heroes have studied God's Word all their lives. I can't say they know the Bible like the back of their hands; they know the Bible *better* than the back of their hands! However, they often confess, "The more I learn about Scripture, the more I realize I don't know."

Don't get distracted by thinking you have to know it all. The Bible is a huge book! It's not about the head knowledge; rather, it's about the heart hunger. Let's always have a white-belt mentality.

**What have you been studying in
God's Word recently? Remember that it's good
to be a lifelong white belt of the Bible.**

Set Free from Sin

✝

After being freed from sin,
you became slaves to righteousness.
Romans 6:18

Have you ever felt stuck or trapped in your sin? Have you ever told God you're never going to do *that thing* again but then end up failing soon after? Do you continue to do what you know you shouldn't?

Sin is serious. It's destructive, deceptive, and distracting. Sin makes it harder to live mission possible. Unfortunately, we were born into sin, but the good news is we've been set free. In Christ, sin no longer has any authority, power, or dominion over us!

Because of Christ's victory on the cross, His death became our death. His righteousness became our righteousness. Will we still sin? Yes. But by God's grace, we don't have to try to beat it on our own. Jesus defeated sin, so we don't have to feel stuck. Sure, we may not yet be who we want to be, but we're definitely not who we used to be. When we run toward Jesus, our old ways start to change as we look more like Him.

What sin do you feel stuck in? What choices will you make today to walk in freedom?

Know Your War

✝

Put on the full armor of God, so that you will be able to stand firm against the schemes of the devil. For our struggle is not against flesh and blood, but against the rulers, against the powers, against the world forces of this darkness, against the spiritual forces of wickedness in the heavenly places.
Ephesians 6:11–12

When you're in battle, armor is necessary to defend against an enemy's attacks. In the first century AD, when the apostle Paul wrote his letter to the church in Ephesus, Roman soldiers would wear protective gear such as heavy breastplates, ornate belts, and showy helmets. There were many pieces to their battle gear, and every part had a purpose.

As believers, we fight in a spiritual war. We are in constant battle with the forces of darkness. When we recognize that we don't fight against flesh and blood, we recognize the need to protect our minds, hearts, and souls. Just as soldiers wear armor to fight, we, too, have armor to put on every day to thwart the Enemy's attacks.

In Ephesians 6:10–17, Paul laid out this spiritual armor. Understand the spiritual war you are in and equip yourself accordingly so you can stand firm.

What battles are you facing lately? Acknowledge whose they ultimately are.

Righteousness and Truth

✛

Watch over your heart with all diligence,
For from it flow the springs of life.
Proverbs 4:23

The rib cage is like a built-in shield that protects vital organs, including the lungs and the heart. When you're in battle, though, your rib cage isn't enough defense for any attack you may face. It's important to put on extra protection for the area. That's what the breastplate does. Without a breastplate, you are left vulnerable in the very places you want to secure most. However, the breastplate is unable to stay anchored on its own. It needs a belt to keep it in place.

God's righteousness is our breastplate. When we follow His commands, walk in His ways, and live according to His Word, we protect the vital areas in our lives. His righteousness is our defense. And when we wrap ourselves with the belt of truth by remaining in God's Word, we secure our defense.

Is your heart vulnerable to attacks? How can you take steps to defend it with righteousness and truth?

Spread Peace

+

How delightful on the mountains
Are the feet of one who brings good news,
Who announces peace
And brings good news of happiness,
Who announces salvation,
And says to Zion, "Your God reigns!"
Isaiah 52:7

Different shoes serve different purposes. You wouldn't wear combat boots while training for a 5K, and there are better options than flip-flops for hiking. As we continue to fight in this spiritual war, it's important to wear the proper footwear for our mission.

To overcome the attacks of the Enemy, we need to put on sandals of peace. God says that the feet that bring good news of peace and salvation to others are beautiful. So often, our instinct is to fight with others, but that's not what He has called us to do.

We are called to fight for God, not to fight against the world. Remember that the battle is ultimately His and that He wants everyone to come to repentance. When you bring the good news of peace to the world, you wake people up to their need for Jesus. And He alone can rescue our souls. Use your kicks to spread peace. How else will people know about the good news?

**How can you spread peace and good news
to others in your life?**

Shield of Faith

✝

... so that your faith would not rest on
the wisdom of mankind, but on the power of God.
1 Corinthians 2:5

Your enemy is vicious and cruel. He's not out to simply harm you; he wants to destroy you. There is an entire war going on, and the closer you walk with Jesus, the greater threat you will be to the Enemy. But God has not left you defenseless. In this battle, He knows all the tricks of the Enemy and has equipped you with a shield so you can protect yourself. That shield is faith.

Faith is enthusiastic belief in God. It does not waver in different environments or situations. It is the assurance that we already know who wins: God!

Without a doubt, the more you live a mission-possible life, you will face moments when the attack feels especially hard. You may want to quit at times. You may feel tired. You may wonder if it's worth it. Rest your faith in God's power, not in your own ability. He will get you through it.

In what area of your life do you need to declare your faith in God and use that truth as a shield?

Helmet of Salvation

✝

The peace of God, which surpasses all comprehension,
will guard your hearts and minds in Christ Jesus.
Philippians 4:7

Have you ever lain awake in bed at night filled with guilt about something you have already been forgiven for? Maybe you blew up at your parents again or said something mean to a kid at school. It can be any number of things that are trying to mess you up, even after you have asked God to forgive you.

When your thoughts are bombarded with lies and accusations, put your focus on the Cross and what Jesus has done. The helmet of salvation is your defense. Remember whose you are and who you are. You are a child of God, saved by grace by the blood of Jesus, who died on a cross for you and rose again three days later.

Tell God all your anxious thoughts. He will exchange your anxiety for peace, and that peace will act as a guard against the schemes of the devil.

**What anxious thoughts are you fighting today?
Remind yourself of your salvation and bring your
thoughts to God in prayer.**

Sword of the Spirit

✝

The word of God is living and active, and sharper than
any two-edged sword, even penetrating as far as the division of
soul and spirit, of both joints and marrow, and able to
judge the thoughts and intentions of the heart.
Hebrews 4:12

Swords have been around for thousands of years. The double-edged sword has two sharpened edges. A highly effective weapon, this sword prevents an opponent from grabbing the blade to use it against the holder.

We have been equipped with one offensive weapon in our arsenal: the Word of God. The Bible is more than a book or history lesson, and reading it is more than a task. God has spoken through His Word, and He continues to speak to us through it as we dig more deeply into it.

When you are in the Word regularly, the Holy Spirit works to drill it deep into your heart so that when an attack comes, you are equipped with biblical truth to defend yourself. Use it to fight back wherever you may need to.

Do you treat reading your Bible as a chore or as battle prep? Intentionally dive into it today.

The Power of Prayer

✝

With every prayer and request, pray at all times
in the Spirit, and with this in view, be alert with all
perseverance and every request for all the saints.
Ephesians 6:18

If you feel alone today, please know that God has not left you. He has not abandoned you to fight your battles alone. In fact, He wants to be in relationship with you. He has opened up a line of communication for you and Him. Use it. Even Jesus, God's own Son, often slipped away from the crowds so He could pray to His Father in heaven.

When we pray, we do more than recite a few words to God. We reach His heart. Prayer keeps us alert and focused on our mission. Through it, we can witness God's miracles. By setting aside time to talk to and listen to Him, He will begin to transform us and work in ways that we never imagined. Don't neglect or underestimate the power of prayer. When we pray, we can trust God to work behind the scenes in impossible ways.

**How have you witnessed God work
through your prayers?**

A Prayer to Stand Firm

✝

Lord, as I make the conscious choice each day to follow You, I understand that this world will not always like what I do and what I stand for. As You have promised, I will face trials and trouble. There is an enemy who prowls around like a roaring lion looking for someone to devour. Because You were persecuted, when I stand up for You, I too will experience some form of persecution.

But thanks be to God, for in Jesus, I have victory! You have overcome the world, and that is why I can take heart, be courageous, and stand firm. By the power of Your Spirit, I will let nothing move me today. I will live by my convictions and not by my emotions. I will pursue respect and not popularity. I will be unashamed of the gospel, for it is by Your power that I have been set free. Sin and death have been defeated. Therefore, I will not be burdened by old sin habits. Help me stay alert and on guard, ready to do everything in love today.

In Jesus's name. Amen.

Based on: 1 Peter 5:8–9; John 15:18–25; Galatians 5:1; 1 Corinthians 15:57–58; 16:13; John 16:33

Take the Bloody Nose

+

I am confident of this very thing, that He who began a good
work among you will complete it by the day of Christ Jesus.
Philippians 1:6

When my dad was called by God to serve as a missionary in
the Philippines with his family, it wasn't an easy road. Moving a family of four kids to the other side of the world was challenging. But because Dad knew he was supposed to go, he tackled each hardship and pressed onward, with Mom's support every step of the way. He kept loving, serving, and leading millions of people to the Lord.

I remember Dad would always say to me, "Timmy, if you know God has called you to do something and you get punched in the process and get a bloody nose, that's okay. Keep going. But if you don't know you're called to do whatever you are doing, the first time you get a bloody nose, you're going to look for every reason to retreat." In other words, if you face resistance on the journey of a mission-possible life, don't use it as an excuse to retreat. Stay in the fight.

**What has God called you to that you
feel afraid to try or do?**

Source of the Setback

✝

You cannot stand against your enemies until you have
removed the designated things from your midst.
Joshua 7:13

When the Israelites entered the Promised Land after a strenuous forty-year journey, they experienced a succession of miraculous victories. After they conquered the city of Jericho, they came to a place called Ai. Up for another fight, the Israelites, led by Joshua, were confident they could crush the enemy's small army. But in a shocking twist, they were defeated.

Joshua 7:5 says, "The hearts of the people melted and became like water." What a picture of hopes dashed! Unfortunately, someone in the camp had been disobedient, and this unchecked disobedience was the source of the terrible defeat.

Setbacks come in all shapes and sizes. Sometimes life happens in a bad way, through no fault of our own, and sometimes consequences come as a result of choices we've made. Remain connected to God. Ask Him to help you keep your motives in check and for the wisdom to remain obedient.

**What's going on in your life right now, good or bad?
Talk to God about it.**

Beyond All That We Think

✝

Is anything too difficult for the LORD?
Genesis 18:14

At an event a few years back, I was approached by a young woman. She was holding a baby and crying. In between sobs, she managed to say to me, "I just want you to hold a life that you helped save." Then she mentioned the TV commercial my mom and I did in 2010.

The message of the thirty-second clip was simple: "Celebrate family. Celebrate life." Through the website that shared Mom's story, this young woman learned that my mom was very sick when she became pregnant with me. The best doctor in their area at the time advised my mom to abort me to save her own life. Mom refused, trusting God with my life and hers. You know the ending. (Look back at May 27 for a reminder of the details.)

Many folks told me that doing the commercial was a bad idea, but because I am passionate about celebrating life, I was honored to be a part of it. Trust that God is in control of your mission. He's got a greater purpose in store than you may think.

Identify a setback getting in the way of your mission-possible life. Know that pushing through will lead to accomplishing God's great purpose in and through your life.

Weapons of Worship

✛

Let the word of Christ richly dwell within you, with all
wisdom teaching and admonishing one another with psalms,
hymns, and spiritual songs, singing with thankfulness
in your hearts to God.
Colossians 3:16

P aul and Silas ministered in Syria and through Asia Minor. On
the men's mission-trip tour, many people were saved and
churches planted. When the duo arrived in Macedonia, God continued to do a great work, but the opposition picked up strength.
Paul and Silas were beaten and thrown in jail.

This winning team was fastened in stocks. Stranded. No hope of
a better tomorrow. But here's what's so cool: Paul and Silas may
have been disappointed, but they certainly didn't wallow in pity.
They prayed. They sang. They worshipped. Then at midnight, an
earthquake erupted, opening the prison doors. Paul and Silas were
able to minister to the suicidal jailer, who knew he was going to be
in big trouble with his employers, and he came to know the Lord.

Praise has a powerful place in our pain. When resistance comes,
make a habit of lifting up your heart to God.

**Take a few undistracted minutes to sing your
favorite worship song a couple of times. This could
become your best tool against adversity.**

Wind Is Your Friend

✛

Rejoicing in hope, persevering in tribulation,
devoted to prayer . . .
Romans 12:12

You might think that violent wind makes for a bad airplane flight. And while that certainly can be true, did you know that pilots *prefer* to take off into the wind? Not with the wind at their backs, pushing them forward, but into what you might call a force of resistance. Common sense may tell us that taking off into the wind will result in slowing the plane down and forcing it to burn more fuel than necessary, yet the opposite is true. When a plane takes off into the wind, it can reach a higher altitude in less time and with less speed.

A problem doesn't have to have a negative effect all the time. It might help you achieve a greater purpose. It might help build your character, open a door of opportunity, or connect you with a person who you wouldn't otherwise have met.

Don't waste all your time bemoaning the weight of resistance. Pray and ask God to use it to make you better and bring Him glory.

**When's the last time a hardship became
an opportunity? What did you learn
from that experience?**

Wounds Get Used

✛

It is through many tribulations that we must enter
the kingdom of God.
Acts 14:22

There are so many heroes of the Bible who were wounded deeply before they were ever used greatly. Think of the trials that Job wrestled with: losing his loved ones, his business, his health, and the love of his wife. Think of Joseph, who lost the loyalty of his family and his freedom. Think about Paul, who gained a miraculous conversion experience but was persecuted and prosecuted for his faith. In fact, many of the characters in the Bible are well known because of the struggles they endured.

You never know what God is doing with your life now or what He is preparing you for tomorrow. If the saints who came before us had called it quits on the battlefield, they would have missed out on some of the most impactful times of their lives, and their legacies would have been cut short. Suffering isn't fun or easy, but it brings purpose.

**Are you or a friend going through a difficult season?
Remind yourself or your friend that the same
God who was at work for Job, Joseph, and Paul
is also at work for you both.**

See Things Differently

+

"My thoughts are not your thoughts,
Nor are your ways My ways," declares the LORD.
Isaiah 55:8

Fifty-three-year-old Erik Weihenmayer has kayaked the raging whitewater through the Grand Canyon, skied black-diamond slopes, and scaled several of the world's tallest mountains, and he is a certified solo skydiver and paraglider.

Erik is also blind. As a boy, he was diagnosed with an extremely rare eye disease and completely lost his vision at fourteen. He struggled to adjust to his new reality. When he eventually accepted his condition, Erik said, "I was able to push the perimeters of what I was capable to do."[34]

The more we pursue uncomfortable situations and experiences, the more we learn to see them as opportunities for growth. We don't always get to choose our adversity, but we do get to choose how we want to deal with it. The attitude, the effort, the courage—those are all choices we get to make.

Is there something difficult or uncomfortable happening in your life right now? What is your perspective about it? How can you tweak your perspective to align with God's?

The Dash

✛

We look not at the things which are seen, but at the things
which are not seen; for the things which are seen are temporal,
but the things which are not seen are eternal.
2 Corinthians 4:18

When I was younger, I read a poem written by Linda Ellis called "The Dash," which focuses on the line separating the year of a person's birth and the year of the person's death. This tiny punctuation mark represents what we stand for and the legacy we leave behind.

Not many of us want to think about our own death, but ignoring the reality that our days are numbered may leave the most important questions in life unanswered.

When we think about our dash, we can live with more passion. We can make a difference and do things that matter. I have realized that my one goal in life is to show people Jesus in the way I live and the way I love. This doesn't mean I always do it, but it's something I strive for.

The ultimate legacy that your "dash" can leave behind is a life of faith, believing the gospel and living in a way that exemplifies Jesus.

How do you want your life to matter?

Be Eternally Minded

✦

Our citizenship is in heaven, from which we also eagerly wait
for a Savior, the Lord Jesus Christ.
Philippians 3:20

One of my most valued pieces of biblical wisdom is the truth that this world is not our home. Heaven is our ultimate home. The fact that life on earth is temporary has been drilled into my heart ever since I was a little boy. My sense of heaven has shaped my outlook and decisions. It's also one of the hardest things to consistently focus on. It has forced me to ask myself, *Why spend a life building up for a place I'm going to leave when I could spend a life building up for the place I'm going to go to?*

These four things last forever: God, His Word, people, and heavenly rewards. Choosing to focus on those eternal things will make a big difference in our lives today. Not the number of friends or followers we have. Not making the team. Not which college we attend.

Live for what matters most in life.

**Choose and do one thing that can help
make an eternal impact.**

Have a Worthy Endgame

✝

Do not work for the food that perishes, but for the food that
lasts for eternal life, which the Son of Man will give you.
John 6:27

One of my goals is to live with a worthy endgame. What I do on
earth has to be worth it in the end. As believers, people who
ought to live and think a bit differently than everyone else, we live
not for material success but to leave legacies that last.

Can you imagine getting to the end of your life and realizing that
you spent those years climbing the wrong ladder? To keep that
from happening, you must be intentional about making your life
count today! Here are two questions that can help you have a worthy endgame:

- *How can I make a difference in the lives of the next generation?*
- *How can I leave this earth knowing I brought others closer to Jesus?*

Use that sense of urgency I've talked about to motivate you to
make the changes you need to make so that you'll leave behind
something that matters.

**How can you use a talent God has given you
for a greater purpose?**

It's Not Just Your Own Soul That Counts

+

Preaching the Good News is not something I can
boast about. I am compelled by God to do it. How terrible
for me if I didn't preach the Good News!
1 Corinthians 9:16, NLT

I remember when I first heard the Christian artist Ray Boltz singing "People Need the Lord." I was a kid at the time, and the song absolutely wrecked me. Although I was just a boy, I began to understand the magnitude of sharing the gospel with others. But sharing the gospel is a scary thing to do. Maybe you're not sure how to communicate the message correctly or effectively. I get that. But the gospel is hope for a dying world, light that can shine in a room of darkness; we can't let our fears stand in the way.

Sometimes I wonder how far I'm willing to go to invest in someone's eternity. Do I share the gospel with the same intensity with which I try to live? While I'm not saying you need to give a gospel presentation to every single person who crosses your path, I am challenging myself and all believers to become more intentional about caring for the souls of others.

**Name someone you can share the gospel with
this week. Pray for that person, and then share!**

Is Your Life an Invitation?

✝

Accept one another, just as Christ also accepted us,
for the glory of God.
Romans 15:7

I have to admit, there's no way I'm listening to people give me fitness or nutrition advice who don't respect their bodies enough to maintain healthy fitness and nutrition habits themselves. If you don't practice what you preach, your words won't carry much weight.

As believers, we invest in things that last forever. People, for one. While Jesus was on this earth, He gave His disciples a command to share the good news, a command that still applies to us today. It is not a suggestion.

We must welcome those who don't know Jesus to experience a life with Him, and we must do this with more than our words. We must reflect Him in how we live—what we say, how we act, what we do.

Think about your character for a moment. The way you treat people. What you do when no one is looking. As you live each day, may your actions, speech, and character be invitations that welcome others into the arms of Christ.

**How can you live today in a way
that invites others to Jesus?**

A Crown That Lasts Forever

+

Everyone who competes in the games
exercises self-control in all things. So they do it to obtain
a perishable wreath, but we an imperishable.
1 Corinthians 9:25

The Isthmian Games was a prominent athletic event in ancient Greece. Historical records tell us it probably started in the sixth century BC and took place every two years in the spring. Sporting events ranged from running and boxing to wrestling and chariot racing.

In the verse above, the Greek word translated "wreath" here is *stephanos*. It means "a crown of victory, royalty, or honor."[35] In the Isthmian Games, victors would have been awarded a *stephanos*—a crown made of withered pine or celery leaves.[36] Paul described this type of crown as "perishable." A crown of celery or pine leaves won't last.

Trophies and awards aren't bad things, but they just can't be our ultimate goal. Rather, as Christians, we should work hard, exercising discipline in all we do, so that our efforts affect eternity.

**Do a little soul searching. What are you
really chasing after? Will it eventually wither away,
or will it last forever?**

One More

+

Hear, Israel! The LORD is our God, the LORD is one! And you shall love the LORD your God with all your heart and with all your soul and with all your strength. These words, which I am commanding you today, shall be on your heart.

Deuteronomy 6:4–6

In November 2016, the award-winning film *Hacksaw Ridge*, directed by actor Mel Gibson, released in theaters. Based on a true story, this movie documents the life of Desmond T. Doss, a combat medic during WWII who won the Medal of Honor despite refusing to bear arms.

As the movie depicts, the Army wanted nothing to do with Doss. His fellow soldiers called him a coward and made fun of him for carrying around his Bible, and his commanding officer even tried to get him kicked out of his battalion.

But all the harassment stopped in spring 1945, when Doss single-handedly saved approximately seventy-five men over a twelve-hour period on the island of Okinawa. Under Japanese fire, an unarmed Doss crawled from wounded soldier to wounded soldier, praying, "Lord, please help me get one more." *One more.* His prayer spoke of the desire to save the lost and forgotten.

**As Christians, this should be our mantra:
"Lord, please help me get one more."
Who's your "one more"?**

A Prayer for Perspective

✝

Lord, let me see people like You do. Let me love people like You do. Let me listen to people like You do.

Help me step outside myself—my worries, my comfort zone—and let me view life from Your perspective, for Your ways are established. Whatever You do lasts forever. Nothing can be added to it, nor can anything be taken from it. Forgive me for doubting Your purposes, making assumptions, and jumping to conclusions too quickly. I can get so locked in on what I think is important that I miss out on what You're doing in and through my life.

As a citizen of heaven, may I work hard today, wherever I'm at, for the glory of God. You are the only audience I should strive to please. Keep me rooted and grounded in Your love. Give me a heavenly perspective as I wage war against the Enemy. Thank You for being constant yesterday, today, and forever.

In Jesus's name. Amen.

Based on: Ecclesiastes 3:14–15; Philippians 3:20; Colossians 3:23; Hebrews 13:8

Do You Have Peace?

+

The steadfast of mind You will keep in perfect peace,
Because he trusts in You.
Isaiah 26:3

How do you know whether you're on the right path? It would be cool if we could take a quiz that could tell us if our walks line up with the call of Jesus on our lives. But I haven't found one yet. And I probably never will.

Still, there are some checkpoints, which I call mission markers, that we as believers can use to get a sense of the direction we're headed. What follows in the next set of devotions are *not* the only characteristics by which you can measure a mission-possible life. While these markers are not the only standards, they are helpful.

Let's start with peace. Peace is essential to mission-possible living. This doesn't mean you won't wrestle with making important decisions or that you won't have questions. The sure mark of mission-possible living is trust and dependence on God. We are given peace not because of who we are but because we choose to trust in God's plan rather than our own.

Where do you lack peace in your life today?
How can you submit those areas to God?

Does Your Life Speak Your Mission?

✝

Prove yourselves doers of the word, and not just hearers
who deceive themselves.
James 1:22

In Matthew 21:18–22, Jesus sees a fig tree on the side of the road. Hungry, He reaches for a fig to eat, but seeing only leaves, He curses the tree so that it withers. The disciples were surprised when they saw what Jesus did, but this was not just Jesus having a hangry moment. He was showing them how He condemned hypocrisy.

The issue with this fig tree was that, from afar, it seemed to be flourishing, but a closer look revealed how empty it really was. As Christians, we can learn to play our parts really well. If we know the right things to say, attend church often, and memorize a few scriptures to post on our Instagram stories, we may appear to live holy lives. But we are called to live lives based on more than just appearance.

We are to be *doers* of the Word. Our actions and intentions should reflect the way Jesus shows us how to live. We are all in, through words *and* in deeds.

**Are you speaking your mission with just your words
or actually with your life?**

Are You Facing Opposition?

✝

Beloved, do not be surprised at the fiery ordeal among you,
which comes upon you for your testing, as though something
strange were happening to you.
1 Peter 4:12

When Moses led the Israelites out of Egypt, they fled to the edge of the Red Sea. A body of water lay in from of them, and the entire Egyptian army was advancing on them from behind. Talk about being stuck between a rock and a hard place! They were trapped and convinced they were going to die.

Though they were afraid, they were exactly where God had led them. The moment was terrifying and uncertain, but it was by no accident that they had come to this place. The dangers surrounding them were real, but so was God and so was His faithfulness. In a miraculous act, He parted the sea in front of them and made a way where there was no way.

Don't be surprised if you are living a mission-possible life and suddenly find yourself in the middle of a difficult trial. It just might be an opportunity for God to work in ways only He can.

**When things are hard, is your tendency to fear
the circumstance or trust God?**

What Do Your Friends Say?

+

Faithful are the wounds of a friend.
Proverbs 27:6

Have you ever looked in the mirror and seen you had something stuck in your teeth, then wondered how long it had been there and why nobody you were with mentioned anything about it? In those moments, we appreciate the friends who tell us the truth, even if it makes us uncomfortable or embarrassed in the moment.

It's important to surround yourself with people who know you. Friends who really understand you and encourage you to live out your mission-possible life. You need people who won't just tell you the things you *want* to hear; you need people who will tell you what you *need* to hear. Sometimes the truth hurts, even if it's spoken in love and with grace. If a friend notices something that might help you correct your course, listen up. Trust that the people in your life are there as gifts from God to help you on your walk.

What's some advice you would give yourself that may be hard to hear but you know you need to hear it?

Are You Using Your Gifts?

+

As each one has received a special gift,
employ it in serving one another as good stewards
of the multifaceted grace of God.
1 Peter 4:10

How many times have you woken up on Christmas morning, opened up gifts from loved ones, expressed your gratitude, and then just left them there in their boxes to collect dust? Hopefully never. Gifts are meant to be enjoyed, even if you didn't ask for them. Now, how often have you set aside and never used the gifts God has given you?

You may be a talented speaker or a really good writer. Maybe you're generous or compassionate. Whatever the case, even if you're not sure your gifts are worth much, God has given them to you so you can serve others.

Are you using your gifts, or are you hiding them? A mission-possible life involves boldness and risk taking. Even if it feels scary, make it a point to showcase the gifts God gave you to serve His kingdom.

What are your gifts? Are you using them, or are they sitting in a box collecting dust?

What Is Your Motive?

✝

Do nothing from selfishness or empty conceit,
but with humility consider one another as
more important than yourselves.
Philippians 2:3

In his book *The Purpose Driven Life,* pastor Rick Warren says that "humility is not thinking less of yourself; it is thinking of yourself less. Humility is thinking more of others."[37]

When Scripture tells us to have humility, it does not mean we should put ourselves down; it means we must shift the focus from our own lives to the world around us. It comes down to motive. Why are you doing the things you do?

In mission-possible living, you can still hustle hard and have big dreams, but you do it with an obedient spirit.

You use your God-given gifts not for selfish gain but to bless others. Jesus was always focused on serving others, so to live a life like He did, we need to mirror His actions. When you consider others more important than yourself, you are on the right track, showing the world the heart of Christ.

What drives you to live a mission-possible life?

Whom Do You Aim to Please?

+

Subject yourselves to one another in the fear of Christ.
Ephesians 5:21

A mission-possible life is one of service to others. But this doesn't mean that we are indebted to people. Even though Jesus was a servant to others and even washed the feet of His betrayer, everything He did was in obedience to the Father, not to people. Likewise, as we live mission-possible lives, we need to be obedient to Christ.

Often, we may be so caught up in pleasing others that we become doormats. We make choices based on what everyone else is doing or take mission trips to whatever the "cool" country of the month is. Mission-possible living is not about blindly following the footsteps of others; it's about living your life where you are today, entrusting your desires to God, and being obedient to where He calls you.

Put God first. Put His Word, His truth, and His opinion of you first. Seek to do His will and follow wherever He leads you. Let Him show you the way to live a mission-possible life.

Who are you most afraid of letting down, and why?

Burn the Ships

+

Blessed is a man who perseveres under trial; for once he
has been approved, he will receive the crown of life which
the Lord has promised to those who love Him.
James 1:12

In 1519, the Spanish conquistador Hernán Cortés set sail to the
shores of Yucatán, Mexico. His eleven ships were filled with soldiers and sailors. Though they were outnumbered, Cortés planned
to conquer the land from the Aztecs. Once every man was on
shore, Cortés had the ships destroyed so everyone knew retreat
wasn't an option. Some historians believe the conquistador had the
ships burned; others believe he had them sunk.

Though Cortés's motives were definitely not admirable, we can
learn something from his actions. When it comes to mission-
possible living, retreat is not an option. Sure, it's normal to get
wrecked when we hit a wall. It gets tiring praying for the same thing
without seeing any movement. It's difficult when life gets in the
way—and it often does. But rather than curling up in a dark corner,
we must press on. Pause, pivot, and find a way to move forward.

Don't look back; you're not going that way.

**What ship do you need to burn to be obedient to
what God is prompting you to go and do?**

Listen to the Voice of Truth

✝

Take care what you listen to.
Mark 4:24

I f there's one thing I learned early on playing football, it was that I couldn't live my life being concerned about what other people were saying about me. There is only one voice that matters, and I strive each day to hear Him loud and clear.

What God says about you is what matters most. When you feel less than or unqualified, listen to the voice of truth. I get that we can't hear God audibly, but there's no mistaking His voice in the pages of the Bible. Here are just a few things His Word says about you:

- You are a new creation (see 2 Corinthians 5:17).
- You are forever loved (see Romans 8:38–39).
- You are strong (see Psalm 18:32).
- You are forgiven (see 1 John 2:12).
- You are created with purpose (see Esther 4:14).

What voices call out to you as you try to live a life of purpose? Instead of allowing the clamor of negative voices to hold your attention hostage, listen to the voice of truth.

**Write down three more statements the
Word of God says about you and speak them
over yourself this week.**

God's Presence over Fear

✝

Have I not commanded you? Be strong and courageous!
Do not be terrified nor dismayed, for the LORD
your God is with you wherever you go.
Joshua 1:9

Fear is a powerful emotion. It can push or motivate you to do things, sometimes even good things, but it will never take you as far as love can. I learned about fear and love from my dad. He taught us a lot of Scripture about fear—many verses that my mom put to song so that we would always remember that God is greater than anything we could possibly be afraid of.

Are you afraid that living mission possible will require too many sacrifices? Are you afraid that you'll never find your purpose or that you'll spend more time searching than doing? And what are you feeding more: your fears, or your love for a God who has promised to be faithful? Remember, God never promised a life absent of pressure, but He did promise us His presence.

Meditate on how to prioritize love over fear.

Difficulties Produce Endurance

+

Consider it all joy, my brothers and sisters, when you
encounter various trials, knowing that the testing of your faith
produces endurance. And let endurance have its perfect result,
so that you may be perfect and complete, lacking in nothing.
James 1:2–4

Human beings were created with a fight-or-flight response. This is an inner physiological reaction that activates when we're threatened or under attack. In a way, we're wired to handle stress. Our bodies' stress response was designed to help us maintain our well-being and meet the demands of survival. Research indicates that stress can affect our well-being in a positive way if we have the right perspective.

When you say yes to what God is pricking your heart about, can you expect difficulties? Yes. But there's more! You will also experience joy, peace, fulfillment, and meaning beyond expectation. Living out the purpose God has for you means that the hard stuff has value. And in this case, the difficult times will produce in you maturity, perseverance, and endurance. It doesn't get hard without a purpose.

**Ask an adult in your life how trials have affected
the endurance of their faith.**

Keep Running

+

May the Lord direct your hearts to the love of God
and to the perseverance of Christ.
2 Thessalonians 3:5

One of the most famous ultramarathons in the world takes place in Greece every year. Since 1983, runners who compete in the Spartathlon must finish the 153-mile journey between Athens and Sparta within 36 hours. The fastest time achieved was 20 hours 25 minutes in 1984.[38] Dean Karnazes, famed ultramarathon runner, said this about the endurance required to run such a race: "I think the first half you run with your legs and the next half you run with your mind. There comes a point in the race where the pain, it owns you and you just have to reckon with the fact that you are in a lot of pain and it's not going to go away and to deal with it."[39]

What challenges are you facing today as you strive to live mission possible? Take a breath. Don't give up. If you quit, you will never know where that breakthrough was going to be. Never forget: God is with you as you run your race.

**What extra push do you need right now
to keep running your race?**

Endurance Produces the Greatest Highs

✝

In Your presence is fullness of joy;
In Your right hand there are pleasures forever.
Psalm 16:11

Mission-possible living will give you some of your greatest highs! Joy. Meaning. Significance. Relationships. Peace. I can think back to every moment God pricked my heart to do something for Him. And though I may not have been sure of how to start or where the idea was headed, I trusted God. Then I took a step forward, then another, and kept moving, despite the pain, struggles, and at times doubts. I can say that every one of those calls on my heart have been some of the best parts of my life. They have provided me with more fulfillment than anything I could have imagined. Were those some hard moments? Absolutely! But they were always some of my greatest highs!

Keep enduring. With Jesus, you're going to get more out of this life—far beyond anything the world can offer.

Think back to a hard season in your life. What joy also came out of that season?

Keep Pushing
the Mission Forward

✝

Not that I have already obtained all this, or have already
arrived at my goal, but I press on to take hold of that
for which Christ Jesus took hold of me.
Philippians 3:12, NIV

Every day we push the mission forward. But not every day is game day. What does that mean? Not every day is a day we grant a sick child a W15H. But every day is a day we get to push the mission forward in some way. This means that every day, we are doing research, making phone calls, setting up appointments, having meetings, conducting interviews, creating budgets, finding sponsors, and so much more. You know what a lot of this is? The grind. Putting in the hard, necessary, and daily work that is pretty unglamorous but needs to get done. It's like practicing the same shot a million times. On its surface, the grind can seem purposeless.

Those moments don't feel like the payoff. But if you don't put in those moments, you'll never get the reward. Whatever God has called you to do, every day is a day to push the mission forward.

**Write about the ordinary ways you need to press on
in your mission. Why are they necessary?**

A Prayer for Endurance

✝

Lord, I pray for a ton of energy and focus to keep going today. You have established a path for me to run on. As I look to You, the Author and Perfecter of my faith, help me remain steadfast and on mission through the hard times.

I pray I can run with endurance and do all that You have entrusted me to do. When temptation hits, help me stand firm. When it is painful, help me remain under Your hand. When everyone else is retreating, help me not budge. This is what love does: It bears all things, believes all things, hopes all things, and endures all things!

Thank You, Jesus, for being the greatest example of love. For the joy set before You, You endured the cross, despised the shame, and sat down at the right hand of the throne of God. For this reason I ask that I will not grow weary and lose heart, for Your Word says to consider it all joy whenever I experience hard seasons, because the testing of my faith produces endurance, and endurance produces growth in Christ.

Renew my strength and refresh my spirit today.

In Jesus's name. Amen.

Based on: Hebrews 12:1–3; 1 Corinthians 13:7; James 1:2–4, 12

A Simple Gospel

✝

When I came to you, brothers and sisters, I did not come
as someone superior in speaking ability or wisdom,
as I proclaimed to you the testimony of God.
1 Corinthians 2:1

When it comes to sharing the gospel, we can get ourselves all worked up. Sometimes we put so much pressure on ourselves to say it perfectly. That's why I love the beginning of 1 Corinthians 2. Paul simply told the church in Corinth that his gospel presentation wasn't perfect. He was nervous. But he said, "I determined to know nothing among you except Jesus Christ, and Him crucified" (verse 2). This is the essence of the gospel. Don't complicate it.

You don't need to know the answers to every question about Jesus or the Bible. Salvation isn't dependent upon your performance. God is the One at work and invites us to be part of it (see 3:5–9).

Breathe. Keep it simple, and let God's power be on display (see 2:4–5).

What keeps you from sharing the simple gospel?
How does Paul's approach give you confidence?

The Great Mission

✝

Jesus came to them and said, "All authority in heaven
and on earth has been given to me. Therefore go and make
disciples of all nations, baptizing them in the name of
the Father and of the Son and of the Holy Spirit."
Matthew 28:18–19, NIV

A t the end of Matthew's gospel, he recorded a charge given by
Jesus to His followers to "go and make disciples." This charge
has become one of the most well-known passages in the Bible and
is often referred to as the Great Commission.

However, I was shocked when I recently read a report by the
Barna Group in which 82 percent of churchgoers surveyed didn't
know the exact meaning of the Great Commission.[40]

As a church, Matthew 28:18–19 is something we should study
and understand the best we can. It's not just the Great Commission;
it is our *Great Mission*! It's what the church is all about: disciples
making disciples.

**Part of our job as Christians is to help each other
know what God's called us to do. What's your
part in fulfilling the Great Mission?**

To the Ends of the Earth

✝

You will receive power when the Holy Spirit has come
upon you; and you shall be My witnesses . . .
as far as the remotest part of the earth.
Acts 1:8

On May 8, 1886, a man named Dr. John Pemberton sold the first glass of Coca-Cola for $.05 at a local pharmacy in downtown Atlanta, Georgia. Originally serving around nine drinks per day in its first year, the Coca-Cola Company is now valued at an estimated $87.6 billion. With a mission statement to "Refresh the world. Make a difference," Coca-Cola, in just 130 years or so, is in more than two hundred countries and territories, making it one of the most powerful brands in the world.[41]

No matter where you go—the jungles of the Philippines or the streets of Los Angeles—the red and white Coca-Cola logo is recognized.

So, what's the problem?

Simple: More people know about Coca-Cola than about the person of Jesus Christ.

We must continue to be witnesses of Christ to the ends of the earth. Make the Son of God more of a household name than a soft drink is.

Where do you share the gospel?

Practice, Practice, Practice

✛

What use is it, my brothers and sisters, if someone says
he has faith, but he has no works?
James 2:14

I remember my first time stepping up to the plate after not playing organized baseball for more than a decade. Off-speed pitches were most challenging for me. Sitting back and waiting for the ball to break demands patience—a patience that I didn't always have.

So I had to make a choice. If I wanted to be a successful hitter in the minor leagues, I had to practice hitting off-speed pitches—curveballs, sliders, knuckleballs, changeups, and so on. Though I didn't master the off-speed pitches, I got a lot more comfortable and confident at the plate by the time I retired.

The more you practice something, the better you get. Right where you are, you can practice sharing your faith, practice memorizing Bible verses, practice being uncomfortable—you name it! As James says, if we're not actively practicing and living out our faith with works, what use is it?

**What's one thing you can practice so that
you're ready when the curveball is thrown?**

Take Courage

✝

They brought to Him a paralyzed man lying on a stretcher.
And seeing their faith, Jesus said to the man who was
paralyzed, "Take courage, son; your sins are forgiven."
Matthew 9:2

The Greek verb *tharseó* means to have courage or be of good cheer.[42] It occurs seven times in the New Testament and is typically translated "take heart" or "be courageous." Jesus used this word four times in His earthly ministry. The first three instances were in the context of a miracle: healing a paralyzed man (see Matthew 9:2), healing a woman with a blood disorder (9:22), and when He walked on water (14:27).

In John 16:33, speaking to His disciples, Jesus said, "In the world you have tribulation, but take courage [*tharseó*]; I have overcome the world." It doesn't seem like there's a miracle here.

But think about it: In the context of John 16:33, Jesus was talking about His upcoming arrest and crucifixion. He told His disciples to "take courage" because He was about to defeat sin and death very soon. By saying *tharseó*, Jesus once again initiated another miracle, the greatest miracle in history: His resurrection! How cool is that!

Jesus has overcome the world! How can you
choose to take courage today?

Who's Watching Your Flank?

+

Encourage one another and build one another up,
just as you also are doing.
1 Thessalonians 5:11

Around the seventh century BC, the ancient Greeks developed a military formation called the phalanx. The phalanx was made up of infantry soldiers who fought in a tight, stacked, shoulder-to-shoulder rectangular position and moved forward as one group. In this formation, their shields would overlap, creating a "shield wall" that made the phalanx nearly impenetrable. When interlocked, the shield would cover not only a soldier's own body but also the flank of his brother next to him.

Each man wasn't just fighting for himself; they fought for one another.

Just like the ancient Greeks, we need people to fight with us. We cannot do life or ministry alone! As the body of Christ, by the power of the Holy Spirit, we were meant to fight the forces of evil together. We need people in our lives who make us stronger, complement our weaknesses, and are willing to go with us to the hard places. Surround yourself with those who will encourage and build you up in this fight.

Who keeps you accountable?

Remember Often

✝

Be careful for yourself and watch over your soul diligently, so
that you do not forget the things which your eyes have seen
and they do not depart from your heart all the days of your
life; but make them known to your sons and your grandsons.
Deuteronomy 4:9

The book of Deuteronomy is one of Moses's last written messages to the Israelites. Though he had led the nation of Israel
out of Egyptian slavery forty years earlier, he would die right before
the people would cross over into the Promised Land. But first, God
wanted to remind the new generation of His law before they entered the land. (Deuteronomy means "second law" or "repeated
law.")

This book primarily serves as a written covenant between God
and His people. One consistent theme throughout is a call to "remember" and to "not forget," specifically where the Israelites had
come from and what God had done for them. Moses made clear
that God's people should reflect and learn from the past.

What a valuable lesson for anyone right where they are! We
should often remember that we are saved by grace and make it a
point to live in gratitude.

**What has God done in your life that causes you
to remember His love?**

Chosen by Jesus

✝

You did not choose Me but I chose you, and appointed you
that you would go and bear fruit, and that your fruit
would remain, so that whatever you ask of the
Father in My name He may give to you.
John 15:16

Mission-possible living is not just for people who are perfect or seem to have it all together. God has a history of choosing unlikely people to work His miracles through. Even when Jesus walked this earth, He chose imperfect people to follow Him in His ministry.

Jesus's twelve disciples were a team of misfits, rejects, and nobodies. He called fishermen, tax collectors, zealots, and others to come follow Him. He was a rabbi, and they, from all different backgrounds, became His students. Many people, past and present, didn't think there was anything special about them. Some of them didn't even get along. In fact, the only thing these people had in common was that when Jesus told them to follow Him, they did.

God is not seeking out special requirements for us to follow Him. He is looking for only our willingness. That is what makes us His disciples.

**Do you feel equipped to live a mission-possible life?
Why or why not?**

A Hesitant Skeptic

✝

Nathanael said to Him, "How do You know me?"
Jesus answered and said to him, "Before Philip called you,
when you were under the fig tree, I saw you."
John 1:48

When Nathanael first heard of Jesus, he was a bit skeptical. "Can anything good be from Nazareth?" he asked his friend Philip (John 1:46). As far as Nathanael was concerned, there was no way the long-awaited Messiah could come from such a small town.

Despite his skepticism, Nathanael followed Philip to see who this Jesus of Nazareth was. And when Jesus saw Nathanael, He said, "Here is truly an Israelite, in whom there is no deceit!" (verse 47). Then Jesus said something even stranger: "Before Philip called you, when you were under the fig tree, I saw you." How was that even possible? They had never seen each other before! Amazed by this, Nathanael devoted himself to following Jesus.

When you first heard of Jesus, did you believe? Or were you a little doubtful, like Nathanael? Jesus sees you, even if you aren't really convinced of Him. And when you choose to follow Him, you will find that He has always known you.

How has Jesus met you in your doubt?

All Over the Place

✝

I also say to you that you are Peter, and upon
this rock I will build My church; and the gates
of Hades will not overpower it.
Matthew 16:18

Simon Peter was always putting his foot in his mouth. He was eager for the things of Jesus but often acted on impulse. On the Mount of Transfiguration, he blurted out words without thinking them through (see Luke 9:32–33). When Jesus was washing the disciples' feet, Peter first refused and then begged Jesus to wash all of him (see John 13:8–9). That same night, he declared his absolute loyalty to Jesus and swore that he would die for Him, only to later deny Jesus three times (see Matthew 26:31–35, 69–75).

Peter was . . . all over the place, but Jesus was not surprised by any of this. He knew the man He called to follow Him. Jesus understood all Peter's weaknesses. And He called him Peter, saying he would be the rock on which the church would be built.

Sometimes you may feel all over the place. You don't have to be perfect to follow Jesus. Walk with Him and let His Spirit fill you. He will work inside you to accomplish the purpose that He has for you.

**How has the Holy Spirit transformed
your weaknesses?**

Sons of Thunder

✛

When His disciples James and John saw this, they said,
"Lord, do You want us to command fire to come down
from heaven and consume them?"
Luke 9:54

James and John were brothers and fishermen when Jesus called them to follow Him. They were honored to walk with Jesus—so honored, in fact, that they asked Him a brazen question: Would they one day be able to get the two most special seats in heaven, to the right and left of Jesus (see Mark 10:35–37)? Another time, they made an audacious suggestion to call down fire on a town as punishment for refusing to accept Jesus.

James and John were part of Jesus's inner circle, along with Simon Peter. Jesus called them the Sons of Thunder, presumably for their force-of-nature ways. James eventually was the first of the disciples to be martyred for preaching the gospel. John went on to write five books in the New Testament. Jesus did not call them because they knew what it meant to be disciples; He taught them what it looked like as they followed Him. Even if you are not sure you have what it takes to be like Jesus, the more you walk with Him, the more He will teach you what it means to be His follower.

Have you felt Jesus soften your heart? In what way?

A Despised Outcast

+

As Jesus went on from there, He saw a man called Matthew sitting in the tax collector's office; and He said to him,
"Follow Me!" And he got up and followed Him.
Matthew 9:9

As a Jewish tax collector working for the Romans, Matthew would have been viewed as a traitor to other Jews for forsaking his people to serve their enemy. He would, however, have been wealthy. Still, when Jesus saw Matthew and invited him to follow Him, Matthew immediately got up. He did not hesitate to leave his riches and go where Jesus went.

Matthew was considered a sinner by the Pharisees, and to be seen with him would have been a disgrace. Yet Jesus didn't seem to mind that Matthew had betrayed his own people before He called him. What mattered to Jesus was Matthew's willingness to leave his life behind and accept Jesus's invitation to something different.

No matter what you have done in the past or how others may look at you, when you accept the call to follow Jesus, you can find a new purpose for the gifts God has given you.

How has Jesus accepted you and given you purpose?

An Adamant Disbeliever

+

The other disciples were saying to him, "We have seen
the Lord!" But he said to them, "Unless I see in His hands
the imprint of the nails, and put my finger into the place of the
nails, and put my hand into His side, I will not believe."
John 20:25

After Jesus rose from the dead, He appeared to all the disciples
except Thomas. When his friends told Thomas about it, he
didn't believe them. Despite walking with Jesus and being told several times by Him during His ministry that He would die and then
be resurrected, Thomas doubted the news. He needed to see it for
himself. He needed to touch Jesus's hands and feet to know it was
real.

Eight days later, the disciples were in the Upper Room. Jesus
showed up again. This time, Thomas was there. Jesus went up to
Thomas and instructed him to touch His hands and His side. Jesus
was not intimidated by Thomas's doubt, nor is He afraid of yours.
Don't be afraid to ask Him your questions. Expect His response.

**What doubts do you have about Jesus?
Present them to Him today.**

Suffering to Salvation

✢

*I consider that the sufferings of this present time
are not worthy to be compared with the glory
that is to be revealed to us.*
Romans 8:18

Guest devo by Abbey Gideon
**Relationship to TTF: on-site director of summer camp
at Rising Light Ridge**

Before I left on a road trip to clear my head after a traumatic experience, I received an opportunity to work for Rising Light Ridge. This is a learning and ministry facility providing a community of belonging to participants of all backgrounds and abilities in Pennsylvania. I had no idea what to expect other than I knew I had to go. After returning from my road trip, I headed to Pennsylvania. I began seeing God work, but I wasn't a believer yet. At Rising Light, God put me in a community in which His presence surrounded me for the first time in my life. Finally, after guidance from my community and praying, I made the decision to trust and follow Jesus.

Sometimes you can't see God until you endure something that causes you to look up. The pain and suffering that I experienced led me on a divine path to accept Christ into my life and continue to grow in my faith. God always has a plan, even when we cannot see it during times of suffering. There is a greater glory that will be revealed to us.

**How has God revealed Himself to you
through your suffering?**

Strength Is a Key Ingredient to God's Heart

✝

I can do all things through Him who strengthens me.
Philippians 4:13

Guest devo by Kelly Faughnan
Relationship to TTF: W15H recipient

Not long ago, I was diagnosed with a brain tumor. I prayed, and I prayed some more. Through prayer, I was reminded that everything happens for a reason (even though we likely do not understand the reason at the time). Although I was afraid, I believed that God had a plan. I also recognized that He had blessed me with a loving family and amazing friends to support me through this ordeal. He also blessed me with an incredible medical team that was doing His work here on earth. I survived.

Through prayer, God revealed to me that because of my challenge, I was in a position to help others who were experiencing similar challenges. Specifically, God blessed me—with the assistance of numerous generous people He had put in my life—with the ability to help children who had life-threatening illnesses. As a result of the challenge that was presented to me, as well as many prayers, God has led me to a great place where I would not have gotten to alone. Strength is just one of the many blessings we receive by being in relationship with God.

What do you believe God can do through you today?

A New Perspective

✝

In this you greatly rejoice, even though now for a little while,
if necessary, you have been distressed by various trials,
so that the proof of your faith, being more precious than gold
which perishes though tested by fire, may be found to result in
praise, glory, and honor at the revelation of Jesus Christ.
1 Peter 1:6–7

Guest devo by Stacie Mockbee
Relationship to TTF: Night to Shine director

"I can't wait to die." My son spoke these words with such confidence that it emptied my lungs of oxygen. He continued to talk about how exciting it will be to see Jesus. "Mama, do you think I will be able to spend time with Jesus? I will have a new body in heaven, and I want to have a race with Him!" Suffering and pain were Jacob's lifelong companions, yet he lived a life so full of hope and expectation.

Suffering is inevitable. In the passage above, Peter wasn't suggesting that we rejoice over our trials and pain; rather, he was reminding us that we have a tried-and-true hope, one that won't fall apart like everything else around us. When we look for God's goodness, we will find evidence of it everywhere! Our suffering doesn't define our stories; our living hope in Jesus does.

Jacob died shortly after our conversation, and I can only imagine what it must have been like for him to leave behind his wheelchair, ventilator, and daily suffering and experience the joy of the inheritance kept in heaven for him. I would have loved to watch that race with Jesus down the streets of gold!

**Jot down some things you know about
the living hope you have.**

A Prayer for Faithfulness

✝

Lord, with You all things are possible! Help me today to walk with conviction, even when things are uncertain.

Give me faith like Noah, who spent many years preparing for what was to come. Give me faith like Abraham, who was willing to go wherever You led him. Give me faith like Moses, who trusted Your power and provision. Give me faith like David, who honored Your anointed even when treated harshly. Give me faith like Shadrach, Meshach, and Abednego, who didn't give in to peer pressure. Give me faith like Daniel, who stood firm in chaos. Give me faith like Esther, who put everything on the line to save her people. Give me faith like the disciples, who simply obeyed Your command "Follow Me." Give me faith like Paul, who was unashamed to share the gospel, even when faced with opposition.

Lord, all throughout Your Word, I'm encouraged by the belief of those who have gone before me. Like those men and women, may I walk by faith and not by sight. May I surrender my plans, wants, desires, and dreams and trust what You're doing in and through me. Thank You for always being faithful!

In Jesus's name. Amen.

Based on: Matthew 19:26; Hebrews 11; Matthew 4:19; 2 Corinthians 5:7; Ecclesiastes 3:1–11

Respect Divine Timing

+

His anger is but for a moment,
His favor is for a lifetime;
Weeping may last for the night,
But a shout of joy comes in the morning.
Psalm 30:5

After defeating the Philistine giant, Goliath, David saw his popularity grow throughout the land of Israel. King Saul saw him as a threat to his throne and attempted to kill him multiple times. As a result, David fled for his life and spent many years on the run.

Recruiting friends and family, David built a small army of his own. When presented with two separate opportunities to kill King Saul, he did not take either. Marked as a man after God's own heart, David respected God's timing. Was he confused by how God was working? I'm sure. He had a bounty on his head for no reason! But in all the chaos, not knowing if he would even survive long enough to become king, David remained obedient. He didn't try to take things into his own hands. He let God be God and did his best to walk in faith.

**Obedience is hard, and we don't always like it.
How does this snapshot of David's life encourage
you to trust what God is doing?**

Your Will, Not Mine

✝

Father, if You are willing, remove this cup from Me;
yet not My will, but Yours be done.
Luke 22:42

Guest devo by Irene and Alfredo Salazar
Relationship to TTF: pastors of Vida Church in Guatemala and
founders of Tebow Down Guatemala

In August 2005, our son, Alfredo, entered the hospital. He had five heart defects, and open-heart surgery was the only way to correct them. There was no guarantee he would make it through the surgery. It was time to put our trust in the only Giver of life, Jesus. The nurse came to take Alfredo to the operating room and told us, "It's time."

We asked the nurse to give us a moment to say goodbye to our son and pray for him. Our prayer was, "Father, You gave us Alfredo, a beautiful baby with Down syndrome. If Your will is for him to return to heaven, we will accept it, but our desire is for him to stay with us on this earth and for us to be able to take care of him and watch him grow. Yet not our will, but Yours be done."

Twenty-four hours after the surgery, Alfredo left the intensive care unit. A week after his surgery, he was ready to leave the hospital and recover with us at home. Doctors said it was a miracle!

We knew that the Lord's will was to bless many lives through Alfredo's life, and we have done so throughout all these years. We learned that the Lord's will is always the best for our lives, even as we go through very difficult times.

Irene and Alfredo were able to use their son's life
as a blessing for others. How have you been able to
see God work through difficult times?

Suffering in Faith

✠

To this you were called, because Christ suffered for you,
leaving you an example, that you should follow in his steps.
1 Peter 2:21, NIV

Guest devo by Tracy Umezu
Relationship to TTF: adoption-grant recipient

I never thought life would be easy or perfect, but the loss of two of our daughters broke my heart. In the days and years following my losses, I turned to the church. As my faith deepened, I was drawn to the suffering Jesus experienced for us (and to the visceral pain Mary, His earthly mother, must have felt watching her son suffer and die).

Living in faith while simultaneously grieving my daughters began to feel like the least I could do for all the suffering Jesus endured for me.

God never promised a life free of suffering, but He has promised that He is with us always if we open our hearts and let Him in. The resurrection of Christ was God's faithful promise to us that through all the suffering we will experience, at the end of our journeys heaven waits for us and we will be completely healed. By allowing God in at our darkest hours and holding on to the faithful promises He gives us, we are drawn into a closer and more intimate relationship with Him. This allows us to physically feel closer to eternal life and hope for what is to come.

How might remaining faithful to God in your darkest hour be an example to others of the strength faith gives during hard times?

Lord, First Let Me . . .

+

He said to another man, "Follow me." But he replied,
"Lord, first let me go and bury my father." Jesus said to him,
"Let the dead bury their own dead, but you go
and proclaim the kingdom of God."
Luke 9:59–60, NIV

Guest devo by Hope Kim Pranza
Relationship to TTF: storyteller at the Tebow CURE Hospital
in the Philippines

Let the dead bury their own dead? That seems harsh, or so I thought. My father had been at a hospital in Florida for months when a ministry opportunity arose in the Philippines. I had questions about God's timing. I felt the same as the man in Luke: *Lord, first let me . . .*

Like mine, it's likely the man's father wasn't dead. He wanted to follow Jesus, but he asked to wait a little while. By "let[ting] the dead bury their own dead," Jesus reminds us that following Him should be our priority.

Convicted in my response, I wholeheartedly surrendered my decision—and my dad—to God. During my first week of serving, he had six cardiac arrests, leading him to his final rest. Thanks to the internet, I was still "present" at my father's funeral as I served at the Tebow CURE Hospital. Answering God's invite, I witnessed life-changing surgeries leading to faith in Jesus. "Let the dead bury their own dead" doesn't mean leaving your responsibilities to your family; it means stepping in faith to obey Him as He invites you to a most incredible opportunity in making His name known.

**What do you need to surrender so you can go
and proclaim the kingdom of God? Ask God to
give you the courage to follow Him and place
Him as your ultimate priority.**

Don't Underestimate the Small Steps

✛

Come and see the works of God,
Who is awesome in His deeds toward the sons of mankind.
Psalm 66:5

In 1855, Edward Kimball, an ordinary man who taught Sunday school at his church in Boston, had a goal to share the gospel with every teenage boy in his class. Concerned about one of his students, Kimball showed up at the shoe store where this seventeen-year-old worked. There, Kimball shared God's love with the boy, and shortly after, the young salesman, named Dwight L. Moody, received Christ.

Moody went on to become one of the greatest evangelists of the nineteenth century, leading millions of people to Christ. But the story doesn't stop there. Moody befriended a college student named J. Wilbur Chapman, who became a famous evangelist as well! During his ministry, he hired a former pro baseball player named Billy Sunday to be his assistant. Sunday became a dynamic evangelist and influenced a group of Christian men in Charlotte, North Carolina.

Then, in 1934, this same group of men invited Dr. Mordecai Ham to host a tent revival in their city. It was there a teenage boy surrendered his life to Jesus Christ. This young boy's name was Billy Graham. And throughout his life, he shared the gospel with more than two billion people.[43]

Here's the point: Don't underestimate your small steps of obedience. Just like with Mr. Kimball, God will use your faithfulness too!

**What small step in obedience is
God asking you to take?**

I Will Not Be Overwhelmed

+

When he falls, he will not be hurled down,
Because the LORD is the One who holds his hand.
Psalm 37:24

Failure is inevitable. It's a given. It's going to happen. And that's okay! Let me be honest: I've had my fair share of highs and lows. I've been blessed to win a Heisman Trophy and a couple of national championships. But I've also been cut four times and traded once. Those lows didn't feel good.

Whether we bring it on ourselves or it's caused by some external factor, failure is a part of our sin nature. But from failure, we learn important lessons. It's what shapes a lot of who we become, probably even more than success does. Only from screwing up and making mistakes do we find out what works and what doesn't.

I believe our *response* to failure is what's most important. That's why I love the psalmist's attitude here. He acknowledged the fact that we *will* fall. Period. But when we fall, we will not stay down.

No matter what happens to you today, remind yourself that God is the One who supports you.

**Fill in the blank: I will not be overwhelmed
by _____ today!**

Closer Than a Gun

+

One who dwells in the shelter of the Most High
Will lodge in the shadow of the Almighty.
Psalm 91:1

Guest devo by Michele Potgieter
Relationship to TTF: Night to Shine host, Reni, Ukraine

One of the robbers held his gun to my head. He ordered me to give him all the money that we had or he would shoot me. I didn't have much. My husband, Ockert, and I sold all we had in South Africa when we came to Ukraine to be missionaries. I took the backpack with money out of our baby's stroller and handed it over.

In that moment, fear came into my life. It controlled my every decision for the next five years. I started shaking every time the dogs barked. One day I broke down and cried, asking the Lord why He had allowed the robbery to happen. He answered me: *Michele, thousands of nights I had been with you, and that night I was even closer. I held you in My hand and covered you and your family under My wings. Not a hair fell from your heads, because I was with you; I protected you. It will never happen again—I am with you.* In a moment, all my fear was gone.

Twenty-five years later, we are still in Ukraine with our five children, testifying that the Lord is faithful to His Word. Though we were robbed, persecuted, falsely accused, and threatened, we are still here. We may have wanted to give up and go back to South Africa, but all glory to God, for He is faithful and gives us strength every day.

The Lord is close to you in your most difficult and darkest moments. Will you trust Him and make Him your hiding place?

Seek and Find

✝

From there you will seek the LORD your God,
and you will find Him if you search for Him
with all your heart and all your soul.
Deuteronomy 4:29

When's the last time you played hide-and-seek? Everyone knows the object of the game: Try not to get found. In our relationship with God, that's one game you won't find Him playing. At times, you may feel like He's hiding from you or trying to avoid you. But that's not the truth. God is not playing hard to get or hide-and-seek. In Deuteronomy 4:7, Moses wrote, "For what great nation is there that has a god so near to it as is the LORD our God whenever we call on Him?" God is near!

Jesus reiterates the same idea: "Ask, and it will be given to you; seek, and you will find; knock, and it will be opened to you. For everyone who asks receives, and the one who seeks finds, and to the one who knocks it will be opened" (Matthew 7:7–8). God promises to be with us. Period. He also promises that when we seek and search for Him, we will find Him.

**You're not alone. As we come close to God,
He is close to us (see James 4:8). Take some time
to seek His presence today!**

You're on His Team

✝

God is faithful, through whom you were called into
fellowship with His Son, Jesus Christ our Lord.
1 Corinthians 1:9

On March 28, 1990, the Chicago Bulls played the Cleveland Cavaliers. In overtime, Michael Jordan led his team to a hard-fought victory, 117–113, and scored a career high of sixty-nine points.

That night there was a lesser-known player for the Bulls, rookie Stacey King. King took four shots and missed each one. But on the fourth, he got fouled. King took two foul shots. He missed the first but made the second. At one point in the postgame commentary, King quipped, "I'll always remember this as the night that Michael Jordan and I combined to score seventy points."[44]

King scored only one point. But in the big picture, who cares? The win was a combined effort.

Michael Jordan would be an extraordinary teammate to have. But when you make the decision to trust in Jesus, you've partnered with someone greater than a stellar athlete. You're on the team of the King of the universe, who makes all things possible.

If you ever start to think your "point" doesn't matter, remember that with Jesus it always does.

Comfort in Trials

+

Blessed be the God and Father of our Lord Jesus Christ,
the Father of mercies and God of all comfort, who comforts us
in all our affliction so that we will be able to
comfort those who are in any affliction.
2 Corinthians 1:3–4

The apostle Paul began his second letter to the church in Corinth by calling God the "God of all comfort." For us, the word *comfort* may bring to mind feelings of ease, relief, freedom, and relaxation. We love comfort and aim to obtain it. It's also empty.

In the *New American Commentary*, Dr. David E. Garland noted that "the word 'comfort . . . has gone soft' in modern English. . . . The word was 'closely connected with its root, the Latin *fortis*, which means brave, strong, courageous.'"[45]

Understanding this idea of comfort should ignite spiritual adrenaline! In God's economy, comfort is confidence despite the unknown. It's a promise that fuels endurance. In this sense, comfort means stepping into the fight, accepting the trials, and saying, "God's got this!"

**When is the last time you experienced
God's comfort?**

He Supplies Our Needs

✛

Look at the birds of the sky, that they do not sow, nor reap,
nor gather crops into barns, and yet your heavenly Father
feeds them. Are you not much more important than they?
Matthew 6:26

I remember on two separate occasions, while I was growing up as a missionary kid, my dad looked my mom in the eyes and told her we had no food and barely any money. In both circumstances, my parents decided to give what they had away and trust that the Lord would provide.

Both times, some family friend randomly showed up on our doorstep. One brought food because she had leftovers, and the other because she just felt that God was wanting her to bring our family a meal.

In Matthew 6, Jesus reminds the crowd not to worry about what they'll eat or drink or wear because just as God takes care of the birds, He will care for us even more.

God promises His children provision. It may not be what we have in mind, but the Lord does provide all our "needs according to His riches in glory in Christ Jesus" (Philippians 4:19).

**How does God's promise of provision
give you peace today?**

Eternal Life

+

Truly, truly, I say to you, the one who hears My word,
and believes Him who sent Me, has eternal life, and does not
come into judgment, but has passed out of death into life.
John 5:24

While studying for ministry, young J. Wilbur Chapman attended an event in Chicago to hear the popular evangelist Dwight L. Moody preach. As he recalls, after the event, Chapman, to his great surprise, was approached by Moody.

Moody asked Chapman if he was a Christian, and Chapman replied, "Mr. Moody, I am not sure whether I am a Christian or not."

Without hesitation, Moody took out his Bible and flipped to John 5:24. Three separate times, Moody asked Chapman to read the verse and answer the same question. After the third time, when asked if he was a Christian, Chapman answered, "Yes, Mr. Moody, I am."[46] On that day, J. Wilbur Chapman stopped questioning his acceptance by God. He finally believed that his salvation was secure in Christ.

Have you ever doubted your salvation like young Chapman? Be encouraged today that God does promise eternal life in heaven for those who believe.

He Will Go Before You

+

The LORD is the one who is going ahead of you;
He will be with you. He will not desert you or abandon you.
Do not fear and do not be dismayed.
Deuteronomy 31:8

When Moses was 120 years old, he was no longer able to act as Israel's leader. Joshua would take over. Though Moses was forbidden to enter the land of Canaan, God's purpose still stood. God's plan for His people was not dependent on any one person; it was dependent upon His power to fulfill His promises.

In one of Moses's last public speeches, he charged Israel to be fearless and obedient because the Lord was with them (see Deuteronomy 31:6). He reminded the nation that God would destroy the Canaanite armies under Joshua's leadership and that the Israelites would enter the land as promised (see verses 3–5). Moses then spoke specifically to Joshua and reminded him, "Be strong and courageous. . . . The LORD is the one who is going ahead of you" (verses 7–8).

As daunting as the task was, Joshua could take comfort in the fact that God was going before him!

The God who defeated the Canaanite armies is the same God who goes before us today. How can you find comfort in this truth?

An Inheritance in Heaven

✝

Blessed be the God and Father of our Lord Jesus Christ, who according to His great mercy has caused us to be born again to a living hope through the resurrection of Jesus Christ from the dead, to obtain an inheritance which is imperishable, undefiled, and will not fade away, reserved in heaven for you.
1 Peter 1:3–4

There are two major ways we understand the word *inheritance*:

1. any money, land, or property you receive after the death of a loved one
2. a genetic trait that is passed from parent to child

In 1 Peter 1:3–4, Peter wasn't talking directly about either of those. He was using the word *inheritance* to describe a believer's future home in heaven.

Aren't you glad that, according to God's great mercy, our "living hope" is guarded, reserved, and waiting for us? No matter what happens on this side of heaven, I'm filled with joy knowing that in Christ, nothing can undermine my and your coming inheritance. May this promise motivate us today to continue to live out the good works God has prepared for us.

As we think about the glory that awaits us, let's do things on this earth that we will talk about in heaven! Name one you can start working toward today.

Coming Back

✛

In My Father's house are many rooms; if that were not so,
I would have told you, because I am going there to
prepare a place for you. And if I go and prepare a place
for you, I am coming again and will take you to Myself,
so that where I am, there you also will be.
John 14:2–3

During the Last Supper, Jesus informed His disciples that He was going away. He also made a promise: He will come again. Although scholars debate how exactly to interpret this passage, the traditional understanding is that it refers to Jesus's second coming.

This was personal for Him. He wasn't just going away and staying away. No, Jesus's preparation was for our sake. Though the disciples didn't understand it at the time, more than two thousand years later, you and I get to anticipate Jesus's return and our future home.

Sure, no one except the Father knows the day or hour of Jesus's second coming, "not even the angels of heaven," but in the meantime, may we "encourage one another and build one another up" as we eagerly anticipate His return (Matthew 24:36; 1 Thessalonians 5:11).

**Jesus's impending return should create a sense
of urgency in your life. How are you living in a way
that makes you ready for when He comes back?**

A Prayer of Praise

✛

Father, praise can be a churchy word, but it simply means to express admiration. From the rising of the sun to its setting, Your name is to be praised above all others. There is no one like You.

In Your name, Your character is revealed. You are my helper and comforter in times of distress. You are Abba, Father, the Creator of all. You are the Christ, Jesus, the Son of the living God, and the Savior of the world. You are El Shaddai, the Lord God Almighty. You are Jehovah Jireh, my provider. You are El Roi, the God who sees me. You are Jehovah Shalom, the very source of my peace. You are the Alpha and Omega, the Beginning and the End, the King of kings, who will reign with love from everlasting to everlasting! I bow my knees before You today. According to the riches of Your glory, strengthen me by the power of Your Spirit. May my life bring You praise.

In Jesus's name. Amen.

Based on: Psalm 47; 113; 118; Ephesians 3:14–21

Unshakable Confidence in God

✝

Rejoice in the Lord always; again I will say, rejoice!
Philippians 4:4

S omeone I admire who always had a healthy confidence in God, especially during the worst of times, is Paul from the Bible. He teaches us that we can find joy and purpose in even the darkest places. That's not only something Paul wrote about; it's what he lived. Paul wrote the book of Philippians, a pretty cheery book, to a group of people he loved. Ironically, he was writing these encouraging words from prison. Some scholars suggest he was holed up in the prison's basement sewage system.

I love how Paul launched the fourth chapter: "Rejoice in the Lord always." While spending time in my *NIV Study Bible,* I came across a footnote that substituted "expressing confidence in" for "rejoice in."[47] While imprisoned, Paul could have written about how anxious and afraid he felt. Instead, he chose to record an expression of his unshakable confidence in God. That's a goal we all ought to strive for!

When's the last time you put your confidence in something other than Jesus? What was the outcome?

J.O.Y.—Jesus Over You

Rejoice always.
1 Thessalonians 5:16

Happiness and *joy* mean different things. Happiness comes from an external source. It's a state of being "delighted, pleased, or glad, as over a particular thing."[48] Joy is birthed in an internal source rather than tied to a specific situation or event. Joy is one of the gifts of the Holy Spirit (see Galatians 5:22) and is found in God. It's no wonder Paul told us to rejoice always.

I like to think of the word *joy* as an acronym that stands for Jesus Over You. When I think of joy in the context of my Lord and Savior reigning supreme over me, over the cares of this world, over my failings and shortcomings, I feel more capable of choosing it.

The only way to choose joy—and keep choosing it—is to seek it in Jesus. He is unlike the fickle emotions we juggle or the shifting circumstances of life. He never changes. He is the same yesterday, today, and forever.

How can reading the Bible ignite joy in your life?

Beloved, Take Heart!

✝

These things I have spoken to you so that in Me
you may have peace. In the world you have tribulation,
but take courage; I have overcome the world.
John 16:33

Guest devo by Janice Tucker
**Relationship to TTF: national legal advocate, victim advocate,
survivor leader for Her Song**

When God saved me, I believed that my life would all of a sudden be problem-free. I began asking myself, *Is my joy based on my circumstances?* As I read through Scripture, I see endless examples time and time again of what it is to have trials and to suffer well.

I am not guaranteed a life that is without trouble on this side of heaven, but I am guaranteed one in eternity. I am guaranteed the Comforter and the Helper in my time of need. I am guaranteed that Christ has conquered death and is interceding to the Father on my behalf. I am guaranteed that nothing happens outside the will of my Father in heaven. I am guaranteed that because of His love for me, anything that happens is for my good, my sanctification, and His glory and that He is infinitely more concerned with my holiness than my happiness. My joy is found in Christ, regardless of my circumstances or happenings. For forever, Christ is enough, and how He overcame the world is enough too.

**How can you be intentional about trusting God
in all circumstances?**

God Will Do This!

+

Commit your way to the LORD,
Trust also in Him, and He will do it.
He will bring out your righteousness as the light,
And your judgment as the noonday.
Psalm 37:5–6

Guest devo by Ken and Amy Ashley
Relationship to TTF: adoption-grant family through
Lifesong for Orphans

Have you ever started to do something that you felt God was calling you to do and then fear and anxiety set in as you began to wonder, *What if this just doesn't work out?* We were in the early stages of our first adoption from China when questions like this one began to keep me up at night, especially when the government briefly shut down and we needed our fingerprints to come back from the FBI for our home study.

During that first adoption, we came across the passage above, which we began to memorize and use to stamp out those fearful thoughts. It truly reminded us to trust God to act on our behalf and bring justice to our cause.

We are still clinging to these verses as we are currently in the process of our third adoption from China, temporarily on hold due to Covid-19. The waiting is hard, to say the least, but through our experiences, we have realized that when God calls us to do something, He doesn't expect for us to do it alone.

**What is it that you need to commit
to the Lord today?**

It's Not Too Hard for God

✝

Behold, I am the LORD, the God of all flesh;
is anything too difficult for Me?
Jeremiah 32:27

G od said the above words to the prophet Jeremiah while he was in prison. The guy wasn't behind bars for doing something illegal or immoral. The king of Judah at the time, Zedekiah, just didn't like something Jeremiah had to say—that Israel was going to be defeated by an enemy—so he put the prophet in prison.

While Jeremiah was imprisoned, the prophecy unfolded in real time. Israel was taken into captivity, but God knew that one day, Israel would be free and return home. God had a plan. He had a purpose.

I don't know what you're struggling with today. What prayer have you repeated for the past few months? I don't know what your outcome will be, but I can tell you that God loves to perform the impossible. It's part of who He is. It doesn't mean He will always answer our prayers the way we want, but it means He is able to do what we think is too hard.

**What do you need to surrender to God and
allow Him to do instead?**

He Forgives You

✝

He rescued us from the domain of darkness,
and transferred us to the kingdom of His beloved Son,
in whom we have redemption, the forgiveness of sins.
Colossians 1:13–14

Regret. Guilt. Shame. Those are some heavy words that make us cringe or remind us of something we know we shouldn't have done or said or watched or listened to. Those three feelings usually come about as a result of sin. Often, we use our sin as our own reason why we can't live mission-possible lives.

Some of the greatest blessings of choosing to trust in Jesus is what Paul wrote about in the above verse: God rescued us from darkness, and He forgives our sins.

When you repent before God, He forgives you. And yes, it is now your responsibility to change your mind and turn away from that sin, but the fact remains that you are forgiven. When Jesus forgives you, He views you as righteous. Not that you are perfect or have finally arrived at your best life, but He looks at you through the lens of the price He paid: His death.

Accept what He has given you so you will have the confidence to share His story with others.

**What keeps you from experiencing
God's forgiveness?**

Don't Get Rid of It

✝

Do not throw away your confidence,
which has a great reward.
Hebrews 10:35

When the author of Hebrews wrote the above verse, he was referring to a particular group of Christians who were throwing away their faith in Jesus and returning to their Jewish faith because Christians were being persecuted. He was begging the people of the church not to give up their faith—to endure and stand even when it was hard.

We live in a consumer society. When something isn't working or isn't the latest and greatest anymore, most of us get rid of it. The author of Hebrews was warning Christians not to throw away their confidence in God. He was talking about a confidence in who Jesus is—that He is the Son of God and that He died for our sins to reconcile us back to God.

If you feel like the pressure is getting too hot, don't cut bait and run. There's a reward for maintaining your confidence in Jesus: You get to live with Him and see Him face to face for eternity.

**How can you feed your confidence in Christ
so you hold fast to your faith and not give up?**

He Is the God of Hope

+

Hope does not disappoint, because the love of God
has been poured out within our hearts through the
Holy Spirit who was given to us.
Romans 5:5

Guest devo by Vadim Martinyuk
Relationship to TTF: Night to Shine honored guest,
Reni, Ukraine

In my childhood, I did not see and did not feel love from my parents. They traded their family for alcohol. After I was taken away to live in a boarding school, I was alone and scared, not knowing what the future held. I lost hope for a happy future and took comfort in drawing and painting.

One day, Jesus Christ knocked on my heart, and I let Him into my life. The Lord began to work on me. He gave me love to forgive my parents. My faith grew that my life would not be the same. I asked God in faith for a new family. Time passed, and the Lord blessed me with a new family so I didn't have to be sent away to a nursing home. In my new home, I developed as an artist and was loved and cared for by new parents.

When I turned twenty, I hoped to get married. God blessed me with a loving wife and two wonderful children. Only in Him is my help! I am so grateful to God. His love and grace are with me forever.

Write about a miracle God worked in your life.

Your Best

+

Since we have gifts that differ according to the grace
given to us, each of us is to use them properly.
Romans 12:6

The science is in: Comparison makes us unhappy. A 2019 study determined that the happier people are, the less they compare themselves and their lives to others.[49] Do we really need a study to tell us that?

All your life, you've probably been told, "Be the best." I'm going to give you different advice: "Be *your* best." Work on your gifts and talents in a way that challenges *you*. Stop comparing your skill, talent, grades, and popularity to anyone else. Comparison will make you want to give up. It's okay to desire to be the best, but it's more important to want to be *your* best. When you feel the urge to compare and contrast who you are with others, stop. Instead, practice positive self-talk. Be grateful for who God made you to be and the gifts He has equipped you with. Work on your weaknesses, and focus on your strengths.

In what areas do you need to cease striving to be the best and focus on being *your* best?

Boot the Bitterness

✝

See to it that no one comes short of the grace of God;
that no root of bitterness springing up causes trouble,
and by it many become defiled.
Hebrews 12:15

Somewhere along in your life, someone you loved, someone close to you, said something hurtful to you.

- "You stink at this!"
- "Why do you keep messing up?"
- "Can't you ever get anything right?"

Those words may have been uttered years ago, but they still echo in your ears today. I know many athletes who have just stopped trying because someone told them they weren't good enough. Instead of honing their skill or improving areas of weakness, they shut down. Some even quit.

If disappointment is not processed in a healthy way, it can morph into bitterness. Mission-possible living isn't possible because we've cemented ourselves in that circumstance. Instead of reciting the negativity, it might be time to let it go. Start listening instead to the God who has engraved you on the palm of His hand.

**What words of disappointment are you holding
on to? What words would God say to you instead?**

A Pathway for Change

+

Was it not You who dried up the sea,
The waters of the great deep;
Who made the depths of the sea a pathway
For the redeemed to cross over?
Isaiah 51:10

When Vinny was twenty-six, he wanted to follow in his father's and grandfather's footsteps by becoming a minister. He studied theology and eventually was called to a Belgian village serving coal miners. But Vinny was a little undignified in his approach, at least according to his superiors. He believed the best way to minister was to live as those he served: poor and humble. He sold all his possessions and slept on floors. The dignified leaders of his denomination were uncomfortable with such selfless sacrifice. They fired him. While Vinny would never enter the pulpit of a church again, he didn't lose his faith. Instead, the rejection gave him a way to work on his art. He'd been sketching while he was in the ministry, and he decided to nurture the artistic ability God had blessed him with.

We know Vinny today as Vincent van Gogh, a celebrated artist whose name is revered throughout the world. Had this famed artist rejected the path to make art and instead buried himself under the soil of disappointment, there would be no *Starry Night*. God can use any closed door to open your eyes to a change of direction.

Name a disappointment in your life, past or present. Then spend time praying over it, imagining what pathways God had or has for you instead.

Persevere

+

Here is the perseverance of the saints who keep
the commandments of God and their faith in Jesus.
Revelation 14:12

I am inspired by Winston Churchill, the political icon most recognized for his stellar leadership during World War II. The man is known as a wartime legend who gave inspiring speeches. A lesser-known fact is the disastrous military campaign he led earlier in his career: the battle of Gallipoli. The campaign failed, and tens of thousands of Allied lives were lost. Churchill was blamed and demoted to the lowest seat in the cabinet.

Churchill was crushed, but he persevered. Six months after his demotion, he resigned and joined the war in France as an infantry officer. He took time to reflect and think of his disappointment as a learning opportunity, all while serving his country and others.

It's not always easy to get over an unmet expectation or a sucker punch we never imagined would swing our way. But we do have the choice, like Churchill, to reframe the experience as an opportunity to grow and persevere.

What is a choice you can make this week about responding to an unmet expectation?

Don't Let It Define You

+

Certainly there is a future,
And your hope will not be cut off.
Proverbs 23:18

Lewis and Clark weren't the first explorers to cross America from east to west. Fourteen years earlier, in 1789, a Scottish fur trader named Alexander Mackenzie achieved this mission in search of the Northwest Passage. He hoped this elusive waterway would flow into the Pacific Ocean via an inlet in southern Alaska. If so, it would open up a new trade route to China and make him a ton of money. Traveling on the river for 1,200 miles, he never found the Northwest Passage. He did, however, reach the Artic Ocean by a river he named Disappointment River. Later renamed the Mackenzie River, it's the second-longest river in North America, as well as a major trade route.

Mackenzie didn't find what he was looking for, but he discovered something else. Unfortunately, he labeled that new thing by what he assumed was a past failure. Don't attach yourself to a failure and let it define your life. Only God has the right to tell you who you are.

If a past failure is haunting you, remember whose you are and let that image overpower the failure.

Why Me? Why *Not* Me?

+

The LORD is my light and my salvation;
Whom shall I fear?
The LORD is the strength of my life;
Of whom shall I be afraid?
Psalm 27:1, NKJV

Guest devo by Jana Watts
Relationship to TTF: mother of W15H recipient who is with Jesus

When our daughter Chelsie was diagnosed with appendix cancer at the age of seventeen, many asked the question *Why?* But Chelsie asked a different question: *Why* not *me? God chose me!* Watching our daughter battle this disease for four years was agonizing. But seeing her faith unfold through much pain and suffering, seeing others find Jesus, was what this journey was all about, even if our prayers were not answered the way we wanted.

Sometimes we have a picture in our mind of how we expect things to turn out, but that's not how it goes. Sometimes we make well-intentioned plans, only to have them fall apart.

Know that even in these times, God is working things out on your behalf with His best for you in mind. Sometimes His answers won't be what you hope for. But He sees the big picture and knows what's right and what's wrong for you in each season of your life. He will never let you down!

How has your journey unfolded in unexpected ways? Thank God for what He has chosen for you, and pray for trust in His plan.

A Prayer for Contentment

✝

Lord, it's easy to always want the next best thing or what someone else has. I want so many things I don't have that someone else does. Forgive me, God! Teach me to be like Paul, who said, "I have learned to be content in whatever circumstances I am." Eliminate my desire to compare. Help me focus on who You've made me to be and what I do have. I don't want to chase happiness; I want to run after You, the God who brings peace and never breaks His promises.

I understand that contentment does not equal complacency or laziness. It means to be truly satisfied because I have everything I need. God, You are all I need.

Thank You for Your continuous provision. Thank You for never failing or abandoning Your children. I pray that fame, greed, money, and possessions never become idols in my life. You are enough. May I be motivated by the gospel today!

In Jesus's precious name. Amen.

Based on: Philippians 4:11–13; 1 Corinthians 2:2; Hebrews 13:5; 1 Timothy 6:6–7

The Measure of Excellence

✛

You are a chosen people, a royal priesthood, a holy nation,
a people for God's own possession, so that you may
proclaim the excellencies of Him who has called you
out of darkness into His marvelous light.
1 Peter 2:9

As Christians, our worth is found not in what we have done but in what Christ has done for us. Through His sacrifice on the cross and our belief in Him, we are set aside as God's own possession. We have achieved the greatness of eternal life not through our work but through His. In this, we ought to pursue excellence.

Excellence has far more to do with our character than with our accomplishments. Coming from the Greek word *arete*, which means "moral goodness or virtue,"[50] excellence is about the way you act, not the things you do. This means that excellence must encompass your whole life.

We live with excellence not to show how wonderful we are but to proclaim the goodness of God. Our aim as Christians is to make the name of Jesus known, not our own name. Remember the measure of excellence as you pursue it.

**In what areas of your life do you need
to pursue excellence?**

Faithful Stewardship

✛

If the willingness is present, it is acceptable according to what
a person has, not according to what he does not have.
2 Corinthians 8:12

What talent or skill has God given you to work with? It may be tempting to look at what others have and neglect to care for what He has given you to manage, especially if it seems that others have more.

Excellence is being and doing your personal best. It's working with what you have. We are all in different situations in life. We have different limitations and are expected to work within them. The goal is not to do everything perfectly but to give of what we have.

If you have time, give it. If you have a talent, offer it. If all you can do is offer genuine prayers, then offer those. Don't look around you to other people. God works through our obedience, not our abundance.

**How can you be a faithful steward of
whatever you have today?**

Whatever You Do

✝

Whatever your hand finds to do, do it with all your might.
Ecclesiastes 9:10

Sometimes people believe that the only things worth excelling at are the things that others can see. But you can't save excellence for the big game. Although nobody can see the training or the practice, if you don't give your all in the things you think don't matter, it won't have the same effect at the big event.

Whatever you do—on the field or off the field—do it for the glory of God. When you study for an exam, do it for the glory of God. When you practice your instrument, do it for the glory of God. Even in the things as ordinary as eating or drinking, do it all for the glory of God. Don't ignore the small stuff while waiting for big events in life to happen. Pursue excellence as a lifelong habit. Remind yourself that the everyday, routine moments of life matter just as much as the major ones.

**Are you pursuing excellence in the ordinary areas
of life? How can you work on that?**

Keep Your Standards High

+

Be diligent to present yourself approved to God
as a worker who does not need to be ashamed,
accurately handling the word of truth.
2 Timothy 2:15

King Darius's administrators and high officials had a vendetta against Daniel, who was placed in a position of authority by the king (see Daniel 6). In order to have him removed from his position, they tried so hard to find something wrong with him, but they could not.

What others did around him mattered less to Daniel than how he would personally act. He held himself up to a greater standard—a God standard. Though others hated him, he was so respectable that they could not find any fault with him. Eventually, Daniel was thrown in the lions' den for his faith, but while he was there, God protected him.

Even when it's not popular, be the best you God has called you to be. Set your standards high. Worry less about what others are doing or what they think of you, and focus more on pursuing your mission-possible life with excellence. God will be with you as you remain obedient to Him, just as He was with Daniel.

How would others say that you are different?

Keep Showing Up

✝

My beloved brothers and sisters, be firm, immovable,
always excelling in the work of the Lord, knowing that
your labor is not in vain in the Lord.
1 Corinthians 15:58

Hard days will come. People will try your patience. What you work for won't happen the way you hoped it would. Your character will be tested at some point. When that day comes and you want to give up and stop pursuing excellence, just keep showing up.

To keep showing up means going to Jesus exactly as you are, allowing His spirit to continually transform you.

Having grit is more than just pressing through in our own strength; it's relying on the strength that God gives us when we have no more. We are instructed to be firm and immovable in what we do. Instead of succumbing to the circumstances around you, remain steady in Jesus. Show up even when it's the last thing you feel like doing. Allow Him to work through you to do what He has called you to do. In time, you will see that none of this labor was in vain.

How will you show up today?

No Overnight Successes

+

The soul of the lazy one craves and gets nothing,
But the soul of the diligent is made prosperous.
Proverbs 13:4

D octors spend eight years or more studying for their degrees. Athletes spend all year training to get ready for the sports season. The world never sees the time and energy people devote to their crafts. Long before I won the Heisman Trophy, I practiced in the middle of the night while nobody was watching. I didn't get to the point of winning without all the hard work that came before it. It takes work to achieve excellence.

In a culture driven by instant gratification and the desire for sudden success, it is often lost on many people that to achieve greatness, you must work hard first. It takes months and years of training, practice, learning, and growing to become an "overnight" success. The road contains twists and turns and some potholes you can't just swerve over to avoid.

It's the same with living for God. Waking up and just deciding to be morally good or virtuous is challenging at best. You need the Holy Spirit to dwell inside you if you ever dream of getting to that point.

Are you working toward your goals or simply hoping everything will fall into place?

Pace Yourself

✝

Those who wait for the LORD
Will gain new strength; . . .
They will run and not get tired.
Isaiah 40:31

When you start living a mission-possible life, it's easy to get caught up in the excitement of living out your God-given purpose. At first, you run on momentum, but soon it begins to dwindle and you wonder if you are well trained for this pursuit. That's when the exhaustion kicks in. Tired and out of breath, you may just want to slow down or even quit.

Marathoners train diligently for their races and teach their bodies to properly manage the distance. Too much sprinting in the first mile will affect how we run in the next twenty-five miles. We can also train ourselves. Isaiah tells us that the ones who run without growing weary are the ones who wait on the Lord.

When you pursue excellence, you don't crawl at a snail's pace either, but you chase it steadily until it is yours. If you are getting tired of running, it may be time to readjust your focus. Look to the Lord and wait on Him to renew your strength. He will refresh you and replenish you so that you can continue doing what He has called you to do.

What does pacing yourself look like for you today?

The Blessing of the Sabbath

✝

In six days the LORD made the heavens and the earth,
the sea and everything that is in them, and He rested on the
seventh day; for that reason the LORD blessed
the Sabbath day and made it holy.
Exodus 20:11

When the Israelites were commanded to remember the Sabbath, they were given a picture of the creation account. God rested on the seventh day after creating the world in six.

Rest is a command, but it has to follow work. Work first; rest next. Rest without work is laziness. Work must come before rest because there needs to be a reason to rest. This isn't about earning the right to rest. It's not about completing a job before resting, because some jobs never end. It's about realizing that there is an order we need to follow. God rested on the seventh day after doing work; therefore, we should rest after doing the work that's in front of us.

Work with purpose. If today is a day for work, do your work. Go at it with all your might until your time for rest comes again.

**Do you struggle with balancing work and rest?
In what ways?**

Rest Is a Command

✝

Remember the Sabbath day, to keep it holy.
Exodus 20:8

The Israelites were enslaved in Egypt for more than four hundred years. They had to labor for others, toiling according to those people's schedules and commands. They didn't get overtime pay or vacation days.

But when God led the Israelites out of Egypt and through the Red Sea, He had a different idea for them. In the fourth of the Ten Commandments He gave them at Mount Sinai, the Israelites were commanded to set aside a regular day of rest: the Sabbath. This was an intentional time to get away from the busyness of life and focus on God, dedicating the day to worshipping Him.

I struggle with resting. Sometimes to me, resting means missing out on an opportunity to encourage someone. But that's not the point of the Sabbath. We live in a hectic world of hurry and hustle, but God called us to live a different way. By honoring the Sabbath, we bring glory to Him.

Rest isn't for the weak; it's for the obedient. Make it a point to set aside intentional time this week to focus on God and simply enjoy the good things He has given you.

What does rest look like for you today?

Know When to Take a Break

✛

[Jesus] said to them,
"Come away by yourselves to a secluded place and rest a
little while." (For there were many people coming and going,
and they did not even have time to eat.)
Mark 6:31

Even when you're going after what God has called you to do, taking a break is necessary. In the above verse, Jesus told the disciples to find a secluded place and restore their energy after they had received hard news. To find new strength, they had to replenish their vitality.

In order to reap any benefit from my workouts, I need to allow for rest days. Those are the days when the tears in my muscles heal so they can become stronger than they were before. Rest days are just as important as workdays.

Living a mission-possible life is impossible without balance. We rest for a purpose. We rest to recover, and only then can we go at it strong again.

**Take an inward look at your attitude and actions.
Where would a break be helpful?**

Stop Striving to
Do What Only God Can

+

Stop striving and know that I am God;
I will be exalted among the nations,
I will be exalted on the earth.
Psalm 46:10

At one point, trainers told me my body was living in a state of
fatigue, which is what I thought was my normal. This was terrible! Overtraining without rest can be harmful. With every training session I put in without adequate rest, I placed more strain on
my body. Without rest, there is no recovery.

In the same way, if we get pumped to live a mission-possible life
and then decide to do all the heavy lifting ourselves, we'll end up
taking on too much of a load and it may crush us.

In this verse, the Bible tells us to stop striving and to recognize
that God is God. We are not Him. We are not as strong, capable, or
knowledgeable as He is. There are some things in this world that
only God can do, and no amount of trying or struggling from us
will change that. Rest reminds us that we are human and have limitations. Trust God to do what only He can.

**What areas in your life do you need
to let God control?**

Don't Miss the Point

✝

Jesus said to them, "The Sabbath was made for man,
and not man for the Sabbath."
Mark 2:27

There was a man who was blind from birth. He would sit outside the temple and beg for money. In that time it was very difficult for people who were blind to get work, so begging was his only means of getting money. But one day, Jesus walked by and His disciples asked Him why this man was blind. He declared that it was so the glory of God could be revealed (see John 9:1–3). After Jesus spit on the ground to make mud, rubbed it in the man's eyes, and had him wash in the pool of Siloam, he wasn't blind anymore (see verses 6–7)! Everyone was amazed. Well, almost everyone.

The Pharisees had one issue about this healing. It was great and all that this man could suddenly now see, but the problem was that it had happened on the Sabbath. They had completely missed the miracle of Jesus because they were so set on their rules for rest. To keep the Sabbath holy is about worshipping God, not the Sabbath. The Sabbath was created for us, not the other way around.

How do you worship God on the Sabbath?

Rest While You Work

+

Take My yoke upon you and learn from Me, for I am gentle
and humble in heart, and you will find rest for your souls.
Matthew 11:29

When we bring our burdens to Jesus, He invites us into rest.
However, at the same time, He tells us to take His yoke
upon us.

A yoke is a device that connects two animals together at their
shoulders and is attached to a plow. In a field, two oxen are paired
together to work—often a stronger one to do the heavy lifting, and
a weaker one to learn the trade. Jesus invites us to take His yoke
upon us. He calls us to do His work, but He does the heavy lifting.

There is work because we are called to do whatever God asks of
us. But there is also rest because Jesus takes the heaviness of the
burden away from us as we follow His lead. He knows where we are
weak and He offers us grace, giving us tasks according to our ability.

We rest to prevent burning out. Rest with Jesus means work, but
since He is with us, it is work we can accomplish.

**What burdens do you need to
lay before Jesus today?**

True Rest

+

There remains a Sabbath rest for the people of God.
Hebrews 4:9

When we talk about rest, we don't mean vegging out on the couch and binging Netflix. Rest can be sitting outside for ten minutes. It can be reading a book. Although it can sometimes mean mindless entertainment, there's more to rest than that. Rest should replenish, restore, and ready us for what's next. It is a sweet gift given to us by God, and it should feel that way. But rest is not limited to our physical nature.

The author of Hebrews tells us that there is a deeper rest that awaits us as people of God. When we invite Jesus to come into our lives and become our Lord and Savior, we receive rest for our souls. We don't have to work to earn the favor of God, because He gives us grace that we could never earn.

When we accept the true rest that the Lord offers us, we become secure in Him and can live from the overflow of His life. With no need to earn His grace, we are free to live out our calling without shame and without bondage.

**How does God's unmerited favor over
you strengthen you today?**

A Prayer for Rest

✝

Lord, help me rest as I should. Life seems to never slow down, and I just try to keep up! Rushing from one thing to the next, it's hard to stop and be still. Homework and lessons and sports—my attention is being pulled in all kinds of directions. I confess, I get caught up in the busyness of my day and neglect our time together.

I come before You, tired. Lead me beside quiet waters and let me lie down in Your green pasture. Restore my soul, O God, and guide me down the path of righteousness, for You are my shepherd, who takes care of me. It is You who breathes life into my very being. It is You who gives me eternal hope. You alone are my rock, my salvation, and my fortress. When my heart is empty, my mind overwhelmed, and my muscles sore, remind me of Your gentle and humble Spirit. Thank You for loving me! May I rest in Your peace today.

In Jesus's name. Amen.

Based on: Psalm 46:10; Matthew 11:28–30; Psalm 23:1–3; 62:5–6; John 5:24

What Do You Want to Leave Behind?

✛

Do not store up for yourselves treasures on earth, where moth
and rust destroy, and where thieves break in and steal.
Matthew 6:19

Having the opportunity to be an ambassador of the Heisman Trophy, as well as becoming a part of the Heisman family, has been a great honor of my life. Still, this achievement did not define my life.

Everybody has their own definition of legacy. For some people, it could mean racking up a certain amount of money or having a wing of a hospital named after them. For me, a legacy is about leaving a big impact on as many people as I can before I'm called to heaven. That is my goal.

What about you? Talking about your legacy may seem a bit morbid, as it touches on the end of a lifetime, but that fact is something that must be faced. It's never too early to start thinking about what you want to leave behind when you leave this world. A legacy is not something that is created by accident; it is built on purpose.

Think of someone who has left a precious legacy for you through their character, actions, or commitment to God. What has that meant for you, and why?

A Legacy of Love

+

If anyone loves Me, he will follow My word;
and My Father will love him, and We will come to him
and make Our dwelling with him.
John 14:23

One of best pieces of advice I can give in how to leave a legacy of a mission-possible life is to love what God loves. What are some of the things God loves?

- the world (see John 3:16)
- "justice" (Psalm 37:28)
- "a cheerful giver" (2 Corinthians 9:7)
- "sinners" (Romans 5:8)
- those who love Him (see Proverbs 8:17)

Sometimes we overcomplicate things and get stuck! We seem to think that only the grandest of gestures matter, that bigger is always better, that our efforts are worthy only if they impact a thousand people as opposed to one. Don't believe these lies. Stick with the basics. Love what God loves.

**How does what you just read change your vision
of what a mission-possible life looks like?**

Giving Always Wins

+

Give freely and become more wealthy;
be stingy and lose everything.
Proverbs 11:24, NLT

The idea that giving is better than receiving is a widely held belief, even by many who do not follow Christ. Giving brings joy
to the giver—a sense of loving, honoring, or serving another well.

The gift offered to us in Jesus's death and resurrection guaran-
tees our place with Him in heaven for all eternity. Because He gave
His life, we have freedom from lasting punishment. We have an opportunity to leave a lasting legacy because Jesus was willing to face
that which only He could defeat.

We are free to give our time, our treasures, and our hearts to others because He first gave us His. As we do, we will find both a purpose and a joy we could not have otherwise known. And this
purpose and joy can live on longer than our act itself, as an example
of the greatest Giver Himself.

**Who in your life needs a helping hand,
a listening ear, or maybe just a few words of
encouragement? Make it happen!**

Weigh Your Dailies

✛

Teach us to number our days,
That we may present to You a heart of wisdom.
Psalm 90:12

When you live mission possible, you are investing in eternity. That means the choices you make today will have an impact tomorrow. One of the biggest ways we see this in action is how we spend our time.

I want to do things that matter, that have significance. As a result, I choose my priorities based on the convictions that God has put on my heart. I want to be the person who follows through on those convictions with my conscious decisions.

We all live no more and no less than twenty-four hours daily, yet how we use those hours is contingent on our conscious decisions. Are you willing to sacrifice a few nights of socializing or a season of your favorite show to reach your next goal? Start thinking about the legacy you want your life to leave, and then make it happen.

**What are two things you do every day
that have an eternal impact?**

Pass It On

+

We will not conceal them from their children,
But we will tell the generation to come the praises of the LORD,
And His power and His wondrous works that He has done.
Psalm 78:4

Psalm 78, written by Asaph, is known as a wisdom psalm. He opened this song by begging the people to listen to his words. He began by sharing the story of Israel's exodus from Egypt—the ups and downs of their journey while God cared for them as they circled the desert for forty years and then finally entered the Promised Land. In this psalm, the writer encouraged the reader to share these stories with future generations.

In this age of instant communication, we can exchange information within seconds. In ancient Israel, there were no memes or Bible verses posted on social media. Stories were not read from books but told orally.

One of the best ways to share your legacy is simply to tell your story. Sure, you can reach many people by doing so on social media, but don't forget about the value of sharing your story in person. It will encourage the one who listens as well as the one who tells it.

How have the faith stories of others influenced your life?

What's Your Story?

+

Always [be] ready to make a defense to everyone who asks you
to give an account for the hope that is in you.
1 Peter 3:15

A person's story is a powerful and effective evangelism tool.
You might think that yours is boring or irrelevant. God dis-
agrees. You are one of a kind. Out of the almost eight billion people
living on this earth, your experiences are unique to only you.

Today's verse reminds us that we must have a reason for the
hope that's within us. An excellent way to prepare yourself is to
write down your story. If you've never done that before, I'm here to
help you.

I've listed a few questions below to give you a head start. Instead
of reflecting on one question at the end of this devo, I'd like you to
grab a pen and a paper and then use the following prompts to help
you write your story of going to and living for Jesus.

- What was your life like before Christ?
- How and when did you choose to follow Him? Or if you
  have not made that decision yet, what keeps you from following Him?
- How has your life changed since making that decision?

You might want to read your story out loud. Also, don't get hung
up on the details. One thing and one thing alone matters most:
Jesus. It's His power in you that makes the difference, not the scenes
in your story or your storytelling skills. Finally, remember that your
legacy is lived out not just in your story but in your actions too. So
be authentic. Be sure your words coincide with how you live.

Character Fruits

✝

The fruit of the Spirit is love, joy, peace,
patience, kindness, goodness, faithfulness, gentleness,
self-control; against such things there is no law.
Galatians 5:22–23

It's said that our character is best defined by what we do when no one is looking. True, but the Bible defines it as much more. It is a life that overflows with love, joy, peace, patience, kindness, goodness, faithfulness, gentleness, and self-control. It is exemplified in its most full and perfect form only in the person of Jesus Christ. As we continue to, over time, live in the Spirit of God and serve, love, and trust Him, we begin to see that fruit grow.

Character is best formed in hard times. When we endure them with God's help, we allow Him to mold us in becoming more and more like Jesus. A mission-possible life is evidenced not only by what you do for God but also by who you are becoming in Him.

Name one fruit of the Spirit in which you have grown since starting this devotional.

One-Up Each Other with Love

+

*Let love be genuine. Abhor what is evil; hold fast
to what is good. Love one another with brotherly affection.
Outdo one another in showing honor.*
Romans 12:9–10, ESV

Guest devo by Kris and Aundrea Whitmire
Relationship to TTF: adoption-aid recipients

I love how the Bible encourages us to "outdo one another in showing honor." Here, Paul was telling the church in Rome that they should do more than respect each other; they should try to one-up each other in doing so. This isn't to be a competition for competition's sake, though. The previous verse states, "Let love be genuine." This tells us that if we genuinely love one another, we'll eagerly and intentionally look for opportunities to honor one another more.

This can come in a variety of ways. We can send someone an encouraging text message. We can share with our younger siblings. We can volunteer to clear the table. We can take the dog out and give Mom or Dad a break. These are just a few ways that we can honor and love each other. We just need to choose to do so. We must be intentional.

**Choose one thing you can do this week
to honor someone you live with.**

Forgive Because
God Forgave You

+

Do not be grieved or angry with yourselves
because you sold me here, for God sent
me ahead of you to save lives.
Genesis 45:5

J oseph's story in the Bible is an apt illustration of forgiveness. Tossed into a pit by his own brothers, sold into slavery, and falsely imprisoned, he had a long history of facing impossible-seeming situations, and none were his own fault! But God had not forgotten about Joseph. After God had restored him to a place of prominence and honor, Joseph found himself in an interesting position. With nearly all of Egypt facing a severe famine, the very brothers who had abandoned him and left him for dead were in danger of starvation. The tables had turned.

Joseph could have abandoned his family as they had done to him years earlier. But trusting God, he was able to forgive and provide for them.

When we strive to live like Jesus, we can do hard things. If we continue to trust Him, God can use whatever has happened to us to work things out for good.

Are you in a hard place? Spend a few minutes asking God for help to trust Him.

Honor What God Honors

+

Everyone who exalts himself will be humbled,
and the one who humbles himself will be exalted.
Luke 14:11

In Luke 14, we read about Jesus being at a dinner with friends. Jesus noticed how quickly the guests, including His beloved disciples, picked out their seats. They wanted to sit in the best places—the places of honor. In those days, where you sat reflected your degree of importance.

Jesus used the opportunity to teach humility. He dished out the timeless wisdom in the verse above that humility brings exaltation and not the other way around.

Often, we're quick to honor what we think is important. Many times, that's ourselves! We decide what we deserve, when we need a like, when it's time to level up, and who belongs in our circle. Self-centeredness is damaging to a mission-possible life. Jesus, divine in flesh, showed us how to live with humility. Let us emulate His example and allow our Father in heaven to exalt us how and when He chooses.

What is the difference between a false sense of humility and the sincere kind that Jesus is referring to in this passage?

Know You and Trust God

✝

One who trusts in his own heart is a fool.
Proverbs 28:26

I'll never forget one time that I was scheduled to give a talk. I knew the gist of what I wanted to say, but I didn't have the time I needed to get a feel for the crowd.

Fifteen minutes into my message, I began to groan on the inside. I didn't think what I was saying was coming across powerfully. I wanted so desperately to give the crowd hope but felt I was failing miserably. Then God took over my babble. I felt Him saying, "Timmy, remember why you're here. It's not about how or what you say; it's about having a heart for these people like I do."

When we think we have power in our words alone, they will fall flat. If God's power is in us, however, the words we speak will never fail. That day, many came to know Jesus.

I stepped into this event knowing God but trusting me instead of knowing me and trusting God. When I remembered that the message wasn't about me, He took my average and my pride and brought many people to Him. I'm grateful that's how He rolls.

**In what areas of your life do you need to
step aside and let God take over?**

Go Back to the Well

✝

Seek the LORD and His strength;
Seek His face continually.
1 Chronicles 16:11

Going back to the well, or remembering who you are in Christ, is important to do when worries or distractions overwhelm you, whether you're bored out of your skull or have no clue how to start your English paper.

Our faith in what God says about us permeates everything we do. When we've lost our motivation, we need to look back and remember what created our motivation in the first place. This is a spiritual practice. Instead of reminding yourself of your own highlight reel, like the trophy you earned or the latest grade on your math test, rev up your momentum in a better way.

Look back and remember. Remember how God carried you through a difficult time. Remember the grace He gave you each time you messed up. Remembering is not about living in the past; it's about reminding ourselves who God is in us.

Tell yourself to take a break from thinking about the possibilities of what might happen or how things could turn out. Instead, think back to a time when God showed up. Then remind yourself of this: As He did then, He will do now, because He is the God who never changes.

Bring Out the Best in Others

✝

Imitate me, just as I imitate Christ.
1 Corinthians 11:1, NLT

In everything we do, we have a chance to influence people. In fact, one of the greatest things we can do in life is influence other people for the better. Like Paul, who wrote the above words, I want to bring out the best in others, from those who are closest to me to those I meet for the first time. I want people's lives to be better because they know me.

I believe that every time we meet someone, their experience of us is either positive or negative. Reflect on some of the most encouraging or inspiring connections you have made, whether they've lasted a few days or a few years. What did someone say or do that sparked growth or gave you the push you needed to persevere in your faith?

Just as we follow in the footsteps of Christ, may we live in such a way that we can brighten another person's darkest day.

Is there someone in your life who has inspired you to become a better version of yourself? Tell them how much of a difference they've made.

Putting It All on the Line

✝

After we had already suffered and been treated abusively in
Philippi, as you know, we had the boldness in our God to speak
to you the gospel of God amid much opposition.
1 Thessalonians 2:2

Tied 7–7 at halftime, I knew that to win the 2009 BCS National Championship game against the number one Oklahoma Sooners, we had to play better football. Busting through the locker room huddle, I told my Florida teammates,

> We got thirty minutes for the rest of our lives. Thirty minutes for the rest of our lives. That's our bad in the first half. . . . We get the ball, I promise you one thing: We're going to hit somebody, and we're taking it down the field for a touchdown. I guarantee you that. . . . We got thirty minutes for the rest of our lives. Let's go!

My challenge to the guys was essentially, "For thirty more minutes, let's *put it all on the line!* Let's give it all we got!" There have been so many times I've had to dig a little deeper for the sake of sports. But how many times have I been willing to put it all on the line for Jesus? To do what's necessary for the advancement of the gospel? That's what really matters . . . way more than a game!

Jesus put it all on the line for us. Are we willing to do it for Him?

**What are you willing to put on the line for
the sake of making a difference?**

Righteous and Devout

+

There was a man in Jerusalem whose name was Simeon;
and this man was righteous and devout, looking forward to
the consolation of Israel; and the Holy Spirit was upon him.
Luke 2:25

In the beginning of Luke's gospel, when baby Jesus was being presented to the temple in Jerusalem according to religious customs,
we're briefly introduced to a man named Simeon. We're not told
much about his life—not his age, not his job, not his hometown.
What we *are* told is that Simeon was "righteous and devout."

The Greek adjective translated "righteous" is *dikaios*. It means
correct or just. One study resource I read defined it as being "approved by God."[51] Simeon lived in a way that his life was approved
by God. The Greek adjective translated "devout" is *eulabés*. It means
"taking hold of what is good."[52]

What I love about this passage is that these two words appear
together. Simeon was both devout *and* righteous. He must have
been careful in what he pursued, making sure it aligned with what
God wanted. May my life, and yours, be marked by these two adjec-
tives.

How would people describe you?
How do you want to be described?

A Prayer to Be Different

+

Lord, I don't want to be like everyone else. I want to be different—not for the sake of being different but for the sake of obedience. When You ask me to do something, even if it might be uncomfortable or something no one else is doing, I want to be willing to do it.

As Your beloved and chosen child, I am called to imitate You—in word, in thought, and in action. This means doing nothing out of selfish ambition but instead showing humility, considering the best interests of others ahead of my own. Today, as I clothe myself with compassion, kindness, gentleness, and patience, may I . . . deny self and pick up my cross . . . be quick to listen, slow to speak, and slow to anger . . . do all things without complaining or arguing . . . choose character over popularity . . . and boldly proclaim the praises of the One who called me out of darkness into His marvelous light!

When people ask me why I am different, may I say with confidence, "Because Jesus has made me different!" for I have been crucified with Christ. It is no longer I who live but rather Christ who now lives in me.

In Your name. Amen.

Based on: Ephesians 5:1–2; 2 Timothy 1:9; Philippians 2:3–5; Colossians 3:12; James 1:19; Philippians 2:14; 1 Peter 2:9; Galatians 2:20

Our Entire Selves

✝

Love the LORD your God and walk in all His ways, and keep
His commandments and cling to Him, and serve Him
with all your heart and with all your soul.
Joshua 22:5

Our mission for this world is simple: to love God and love others. To love others, we must love God first. The Bible instructs us how to do that. It goes beyond what we can do for God. It starts deeper, in areas that no one can see, in the quiet recesses of your inner self. It is from those places that we are required to love the Lord.

We are multifaceted beings. We are more than our physical bodies, our minds, or even our spirits. We are comprised of different parts, all equally important in our service to God. To love Him fully, we must love with all our lives. When we keep every part of our lives in check, we will be in better shape—emotionally, physically, and spiritually—to run the race set before us.

What is the healthiest part of your life?
What area needs some fine-tuning?

Money

✝

Honor the LORD from your wealth,
And from the first of all your produce.
Proverbs 3:9

I learned a lot from my parents about honoring God with one's money. Growing up in a missionary family, I witnessed their frugal habits as they supported a family on next to nothing. I also witnessed their extreme generosity, trusting God and giving to Him and others even when they had little left to afford a meal.

When they didn't have much, Mom and Dad gave to God first, trusting that He would provide for their needs. In every season, He remained faithful to our family. Mom and Dad lived with open hands and taught me, through their example, how to live that way too. Instead of holding on to what I own or spending frivolously, I believe in giving and investing.

It's never too early to begin to think about finances. Stewardship has to do with your ability to handle what you are given, regardless of how much it is. The best place to start is to decide to trust God with and glorify Him with your finances.

What's something positive you've learned about money from your parents, a teacher, or a mentor?

Strength and Vitality

+

I am still as strong today as I was on the day Moses sent me;
as my strength was then, so my strength is now,
for war and for going out and coming in.
Joshua 14:11

Caleb was ready to fight for the Promised Land, both when he spied it out the first time (see Numbers 13–14) and when he approached Joshua about it again over forty years later (see Joshua 14:6–15). Though Caleb was more than eighty years old the second time, he insisted he was just as strong as he'd been four decades earlier. He still trusted God to fulfill His promise, and he was ready for the mission.

Get into the habit of caring for your body now if you want to stay on the track of good health. Just like anything in life, it won't guarantee you'll tackle and defeat an enemy army, but it will give you a chance at better physical living.

Eat whole foods as often as you can. Stay away from processed junk. And exercise regularly. You have only one body. Making healthy choices today could mean that, like Caleb, you can continue to do what God is calling you to do decades from now.

**What healthy choices can you make
for your body today?**

Emotional Check-in

✝

The news about Him was spreading even farther,
and large crowds were gathering to hear Him and to be healed
of their sicknesses. But Jesus Himself would often slip away
to the wilderness and pray.
Luke 5:15–16

Do you follow Jesus's example and make room for moments alone with the Father? Instead of getting caught up in everything that needs to be done, it's important to step aside. Often, it seems impossible to find a moment in your hectic life to step away from the noise and get alone with God. So do it on purpose. Use those times to check in on your own emotional needs. Assess your joy and stress levels, your energy, and your spiritual charge. While you can't build a mission-possible life on laziness and a refusal to go, you also cannot pursue it if you are burned out.

It bears repeating: *You are human.* You don't have to be God—you can leave that part to Him. Tune in to your emotional needs by turning to Jesus. By being aware of your own limitations, you will understand how to help other people in theirs.

**How has your emotional health been
over the past few weeks?**

A Clear Mind

✝

Let's not sleep as others do,
but let's be alert and sober.
1 Thessalonians 5:6

E very time you think, you are sending information through billions of neurons in your brain at an astounding 268 miles per hour.[53] In an age when we have access to tons of information at our fingertips, our minds can work overtime. It can be tempting to shut our brains off just to quiet the noise.

However, the Bible tells us not to always be mentally asleep but be alert and sober, or to have a clear mind. God has placed us here with a purpose, and we can't allow our minds to stray. In a world clouded with skepticism, doubt, and half-truths, we must stay focused.

To strengthen our minds, we need to exercise them. Critical thinking is a muscle that we need to work out. Read your Bible, first and foremost, but also take advantage of other resources. Read books, listen to podcasts, and watch sermons. Join Bible studies and discussion groups. Keep your eyes open and your mind sharp.

**What can you do to exercise your intellect
over the next week?**

Step Away

✛

Do not merely look out for your own personal interests,
but also for the interests of others.
Philippians 2:4

It's easy to get so caught up in our own mental funk that we forget
that those around us are also going through hard times. Sometimes we just need to stop, step outside ourselves, pay attention to
the world around us, and do something, no matter how small, to
lighten someone's load.

Think simple. Send an encouraging text to a friend. Take time to
listen, really listen, to someone. Instead of constantly talking about
your problems, find out what a friend is going through. Pray for
someone instead of always asking that person to pray for you.

A mission-possible life aims to put others before ourselves.

**Who are the people around you right now
who could use your love, service,
encouragement, and prayer?**

Perspective Shift

✛

God is not unjust so as to forget your work and the love
which you have shown toward His name, by having
served and by still serving the saints.
Hebrews 6:10

I was blessed to bring Kelly Faughnan to the College Football
Awards ceremony in my senior year. We had lost to Alabama the
week before, and I had been feeling pretty bummed. But when I met
Kelly, my attitude changed. Kelly had multiple brain tumors that
affected how her entire body worked. She was fighting so hard to
just walk. For the first time in a long time, I wasn't focused on me. I
was actually thinking about someone else.

The awards show started and they announced the first award. I
didn't win it. *It's okay. Tonight's about Kelly.* But as the night wore on
and awards came and went, I still hadn't won any. I started getting
grumpy. My mom, who was sitting behind me, leaned up and whis-
pered in my ear, "You've already won tonight. You just don't get
your reward until heaven." Mom was right.

When we aim to live mission possible, what will make our life
count is the impact we have on others. Serving others is central to
our mission.

**What does winning look like
in your life in light of your mission?**

Turning an
Inward Gospel Out

+

Proclaim the good news of His salvation from day to day.
Tell of His glory among the nations,
His wonderful deeds among all the peoples.
Psalm 96:2–3

I have found that reaching out to others is an important part of staying grounded. It's who we are and what we are meant to do. The church is not just a four-walled structure where we sit for an hour or two every Sunday. It is more than a building, more than a label, more than what we do or where we go.

The church is a living and moving body of believers, a body that reaches out to the community as an extension of Jesus. We cannot love God without loving and caring for others.

We cannot just sit in our pews and wait for people to show up at our doors asking for help. We must leave our nests and meet people where they are. Begin by sharing your faith with others. Be an example. Share the good news. Be the difference maker who can show others that a life lived for Jesus is a life that counts.

**What are two ways in your Christian life you
can shift your focus from getting to giving?**

Get a Helper's High

✦

Give, and it will be given to you.
Luke 6:38

The term *helper's high* was coined in the late 1980s, when reports confirmed that serving others produces positive emotions. And the studies kept coming. Research in neuroscience and psychology continues to support the theory that helping others brings happiness our way.

When we feel depressed, lonely, sad, or disappointed, our impulse is to wallow in those feelings. But when we shift our focus onto others and selflessly do something for someone else, our own spirits get lifted in the process. We get a helper's high!

I'm not saying that donating money or helping a stranger is going to forever eliminate all negative feelings. But when those negative feelings arrive, fight the funk by helping someone else. Helping others fosters a spirit of gratitude. It pushes you outside your bubble and into the dynamic tapestry of humanity. It increases positivity and boosts your own well-being. Truly, it's a beautiful thing.

Write about your own experiences of the helper's high. What did it feel like? If you haven't experienced it, imagine what it might be like!

Love Your Neighbor

+

You shall love the Lord your God with all your heart,
and with all your soul, and with all your strength, and
with all your mind; and your neighbor as yourself.
Luke 10:27

A lawyer once asked Jesus a load of questions. In response to His commandment to love your neighbor, the lawyer asked Jesus, "Who is my neighbor?" Jesus responded by telling him the story about the good Samaritan.

It goes something like this: A Jewish traveler was robbed, beaten, and left for dead on the side of the road. A Jewish priest came by but did nothing. A second man, a Levite or temple worker, passed the dying man and he, too, walked right by. Finally, a Samaritan man came by. Although, culturally, tensions ran high between Samaritans and Jews, the Samaritan man helped the injured Jewish man (see Luke 10:25–37).

To whom are you supposed to show neighborly love? *Everyone.*

**Ask God to open your eyes to seeing the
neighbor you ought to love whom you may
have been avoiding.**

Selfless for
the Wrong Reasons

✝

Freely you received, freely give.
Matthew 10:8

I often talk about how feelings can lure us away from doing what we're supposed to do. If we're tired, cranky, or on edge, it's hard to do the right thing. But sometimes there's a different kind of battle at play: a fight to do the *right* thing for the *right* reasons.

Have you ever given much thought as to why service to others is important? The ultimate why, of course, is to do it out of the love God has shown us. Jesus gave His life for us in the ultimate sacrifice of good for humanity. As His followers, what a perfect example to imitate!

Jesus made it clear that doing the right thing for the wrong reason is unacceptable. In Matthew 6:5, He called out people who made a show out of praying "so that they will be seen by people." He even called them hypocrites!

Model the same selfless humility as Jesus to freely give as you have freely received.

**What would it look like for you to serve for
the right reasons?**

It's Always the Right Time

+

Make the most of every opportunity in these evil days.
Ephesians 5:16, NLT

Night to Shine is an unforgettable prom night experience, centered on God's love, for people with special needs. Our foundation has been partnering with churches all over the world to honor these kings and queens since 2014. It's my favorite night of the year. But our commitment to serve people with special needs doesn't start and stop with Night to Shine. We serve people with special needs on a regular basis through other initiatives, partnership, and prayer.

Having a heart for other people means more than showing up once or twice a year in a soup kitchen or helping build a home for a family in need. I love the mission statement of our foundation's president, Steve Biondi: "Wake up. Serve. Repeat."

Do it once, do it twice, and keep doing it over and over again.

Don't wait for a special opportunity to put your needs aside and care for someone else. It's always the right time to do what's right for others.

What are you using as an excuse for not serving others? How can you move toward making the most of your time?

Thanks in the Loss

+

Do not be anxious about anything,
but in everything by prayer and pleading with thanksgiving
let your requests be made known to God.
Philippians 4:6

When I was younger, my mom would always tell me, "Thank the Lord. Give it to Him." She wouldn't necessarily tell me this when things were going well; it was when I was bummed, like when I lost a game. It feels unnatural to thank the Lord when you feel low, but there's an important lessons here. I make it a point, even now in my low moments, to say thank You to God and give my loss to Him.

When we thank God in whatever we are going through, we remind ourselves that life isn't about what we can control; it's about giving up our control to Him.

The very things that don't go your way may be the very things pointing you back to Jesus. Whatever you're going through today, instead of getting worried or anxious, thank the Lord for it. Give it to Him. The Bible tells us that when we present our prayers to God with thanksgiving, He gives us peace that we can't understand. That's a pretty good trade up.

**When was the last time you thanked God
after a loss? How did that affect your spirit?**

What's (Or Rather *Who's*) Your Edge?

✝

I am the LORD your God who takes hold of your right hand,
Who says to you, "Do not fear, I will help you."
Isaiah 41:13

Typically, when you the hear the word *edge* in sports, you think of that *thing* that gives you a leg up on your competition. Maybe it's the fact that your team is naturally more gifted than the other or you have home-field advantage.

I've had so many things that pushed me to be the best I could be. Whether it was wanting to beat our college rivals (Florida State and Georgia) or working as hard as I could to gain the respect of my teammates, there's always been something I keep in my mind to give me an edge.

But far greater than any possible chip on my shoulder or simple inspirational tactic, having a personal relationship with the God of the universe is the ultimate edge! This is a much-needed reminder that God is our source of help, strength, and guidance. You can find many good motivations in life, but when you know Jesus, your confidence is ultimately rooted in His presence and power.

Identify your edge. What or who motivates you?

A Different Kind of Edge

+

The LORD is my strength and my shield;
My heart trusts in Him, and I am helped;
Therefore my heart triumphs,
And with my song I shall thank Him.
Psalm 28:7

In yesterday's devo, I explained the idea of an edge as a motivational driver that gives you confidence. However, a different way to think about an edge is as a barrier—an imaginary wall that hinders you from becoming your best. That kind of edge is that line you don't want to cross because it's hard. It's an obstacle that requires you to push past your comfort zone.

Most people refuse to find their edge because they don't want to come close to pain, vulnerability, or failure. They shut down when they get pressed.

I don't know what your edge is, but what I love about the concept is that it's a key personal-decision point. If you've reached the end of your natural ability, you can *choose* to do whatever it takes to get better.

Be reminded today that breakthrough is possible. When obstacles come, choose to put in the work and trust God to help you do the rest.

**What's holding you back from maximizing
your God-given potential?**

Understand the Gift of Salvation

+

God demonstrates His own love toward us, in that while
we were still sinners, Christ died for us.
Romans 5:8

If you were to count all the ways that you've been disobedient to God, how long would the list be? Mine would be long enough to keep me away from Him for all eternity. All of ours would be!

But because of Jesus, that list does not exist. While we were still sinners, Christ willingly died because our salvation was that important to Him. He restored our relationship with God, and if we believe in Him, we get to live with Him forever. No list of debts, however long, can get in the way of that eternity.

As we begin to discuss gratitude, there's no better place to start than with that concept. This is not a religion that offers course correction. When we choose to trust in Jesus, we're not just going from average to good; we are becoming new creations. Let this sink in. It truly is good news.

**Write God a love letter, thanking Him
for your salvation and for making the
greatest trade in history.**

Perspective Is Everything

+

As you have received Christ Jesus the Lord, so walk in Him,
having been firmly rooted and now being built up in Him and
established in your faith . . . and overflowing with gratitude.
Colossians 2:6–7

Have you ever played a mystery photo game? You must figure
out the image in a photo that has been zoomed in on to the
nth degree. For instance, a black-and-white photo of a surface
speckled with holes could actually be a sponge.

Gratitude is about perspective. If you look at the particulars of
your life today, you may not feel very grateful. Maybe there's trouble at home. Maybe you're dealing with illness. Sometimes you
need to step back and take a distanced view of your life to see the
goodness that has already seeped through it.

Think about the love Jesus has for you. The grace that's available
to you each and every time you mess up. The promise that God will
never leave nor forsake you. Keep zooming out to the full picture of
your life until your perspective turns to thankfulness.

**Name one thing God has done for you this week
that you are thankful for.**

The Source of Contentment

✛

I have learned to be content
in whatever circumstances I am.
Philippians 4:11

When I was fifteen, I went on my first international mission trip. Although we didn't have a lot growing up, I saw a level of poverty I'd never seen before. I'll never forget visiting an orphanage filled with children who had been abandoned or whose parents had died. There was no doubt that these kids, some of whom were my age, encountered more tragedy than most people have in their lifetimes. Still, there was something special about them. They were happy. They had joy. They were content.

Do you know the secret to being content? Paul said that he *learned* how to be content in all circumstances. He went on to say that because of Christ, he could get by with a little or a lot because He gives him strength to endure. Paul said this from a dirty old prison cell in which he was locked up for having shared the gospel. He knew that true joy did not come from his situation but from Jesus alone.

Whatever you're going through today, thank Jesus that He is with you.

**In what areas of your life do you feel
the most content? Why?**

All Your Needs

✝

My God will supply all your needs according to
His riches in glory in Christ Jesus.
Philippians 4:19

When the Israelites were wandering in the desert before arriving in the Promised Land, God provided their every need. Even food. He gave them manna. Now, manna wasn't a typical food in those days. You couldn't grow it in your vegetable garden or buy it at your local supermarket. The fact that manna was there at all was proof of God's provision. The Bible tells us that every morning, manna would appear with the dew. There would always be exactly enough food per household, according to their exact needs. If anyone tried to hoard some for the next day, it would spoil.

But the Israelites got tired of manna. They wanted the foods they had eaten while they were slaves in Egypt. Though they were free and safe, all they could think about were the meals that they did *not* have.

When you set your mind on what you don't have, you miss what God has for you now. Instead of whining about manna, be thankful for the provision He has already blessed you with.

How can you shift from complaining to gratitude?

Gratitude: A Posture
of the Heart

+

In everything give thanks;
for this is the will of God for you in Christ Jesus.
1 Thessalonians 5:18

According to a study by the University of Southern California, people who make a habit of thankfulness are generally less stressed, less tense, and have better relationships.[54] That's just one of many studies that show the benefits of gratitude.

By taking a moment every day to name just three things you're grateful for, you can shift your perspective to all the good happening in your life. It could be as simple as hearing the birds outside or as huge as winning that championship game. The actual thing itself is less important than the attitude of your heart toward it.

When we practice gratefulness daily, we do more than just say thank you. We actually become healthier and more joyful, which leads to even more abundant mission-possible lives.

Start living with that intentional mindset today.

Name three things you are grateful for today.

A Prayer of Gratitude

✝

I will give thanks to the LORD with all my heart;
I will tell of all Your wonders.
Psalm 9:1

As we reach the end of this devotional, in the space below, list specific things you would like to thank God for. When you're finished, like David in the psalm quoted above, lift them up in prayer and praise, for it is because of Christ, and Christ alone, that we may live in peace with humility, joy, and gratitude.

- _____

- _____

- _____

- _____

- _____

Let the peace of Christ rule in your hearts, since as members of one body you were called to peace. And be thankful. Let the message of Christ dwell among you richly as you teach and admonish one another with all wisdom through psalms, hymns, and songs from the Spirit, singing to God with gratitude in your hearts. And whatever you do, whether in word or deed, do it all in the name of the Lord Jesus, giving thanks to God the Father through him. (Colossians 3:15–17, NIV)

A Final Word

Thank you so much for spending time with God this past year by reading these devotions. My prayer is that you've learned a lot, discovered ways to find purpose even in hard spaces, and have powered on a faith that will continue to grow stronger.

This isn't the end, of course; this is just the beginning. I hope you see the limitless potential of opportunity that awaits when you surrender to God and begin to live mission possible.

Don't stop now—you got this!

Notes

1. Robert L. Thomas, *New American Standard Exhaustive Concordance of the Bible: Hebrew-Aramaic and Greek Dictionaries*, rev. ed. (Anaheim, CA: Lockman Foundation, 1998), www.biblestudytools.com/lexicons/greek/nas/poiema.html.

2. *Dictionary*, s.v. "purpose," www.dictionary.com/browse/purpose#.

3. Anne Craig, "Discovery of 'Thought Worms' Opens Window to the Mind," *Queen's Gazette*, July 13, 2020, www.queensu.ca/gazette/stories/discovery-thought-worms-opens-window-mind.

4. *The Britannica Dictionary*, s.v. "mission," www.learnersdictionary.com/definition/mission.

5. In my research, I've seen the Latin origin of *passion* get attributed to both the twelfth and thirteenth centuries. I don't think we know the exact dating. *Online Etymology Dictionary*, s.v. "passion," www.etymonline.com/word/passion.

6. Martin Luther King, Jr., The Martin Luther King, Jr. Research and Education Institute, "'Facing the Challenge of a New Age,' Address Delivered at the First Annual Institute on Nonviolence and Social Change," Stanford University (Montgomery, AL: Montgomery Improvement Association, 1956), https://kinginstitute.stanford.edu/king-papers/documents/facing-challenge-new-age-address-delivered-first-annual-institute-nonviolence.

7. Thomas, *New American Standard*, https://biblehub.com/greek/5056.htm.

8. Rodd Wagner, "Have We Learned the Alcoa 'Keystone Habit' Lesson?," *Forbes*, January 22, 2019, www.forbes.com/sites/roddwagner/2019/01/22/have-we-learned-the-alcoa-keystone-habit-lesson/?sh=660fe15458ba.

9. James Clear, "How Long Does It Actually Take to Form a New Habit? (Backed by Science)," *James Clear*, https://jamesclear.com/new-habit.

10. Healthline, "How Long Does It Take for a New Behavior to Become Automatic?," www.healthline.com/health/how-long-does-it-take-to-form-a-habit#takeaway.

11. David Jeremiah, "Believe: Get Your Mind Right," *Sermons.love*, 2022, https://sermons.love/david-jeremiah/6972-david-jeremiah -believe-get-your-mind-right.html.

12. *Dictionary*, s.v. "ambassador," www.dictionary.com/browse/ ambassador.

13. *Dictionary*, s.v. "rescue," www.dictionary.com/browse/rescue.

14. *Britannica*, "carpe diem," May 7, 2021, www.britannica.com/topic/ carpe-diem.

15. SnowBrains, "Brain Post: How Far Does the Average Human Walk in a Lifetime?," May 18, 2020, https://snowbrains.com/brain-post -how-far-does-the-average-human-walk-in-a-lifetime.

16. Douglas R. Satterfield, "The Fog of War and Other Things," *The Leader Maker*, September 30, 2020, www.theleadermaker.com/ the-fog-of-war-and-other-things.

17. Indrani Basu, "Meet Nischal Narayanam, India's Youngest Chartered Accountant," *Huffpost*, July 23, 2015, www.huffpost.com/ archive/in/entry/nischal-narayanam-ca_n_7855452.

18. Josh McDowell and Sean McDowell, *More Than a Carpenter* (Wheaton, IL: Tyndale, 2011), 155–56.

19. Thomas, *New American Standard*, https://biblehub.com/greek/40 .htm.

20. Billy Graham, *The Journey: Living by Faith in an Uncertain World* (Nashville: Thomas Nelson, 2007), 21.

21. Harold W. Hoehner, "Ephesians," *The Bible Knowledge Commentary: An Exposition of the Scriptures*, ed. J. F. Walvoord and R. B. Zuck, vol. 2 (Wheaton, IL: Victor, 1985), 623.

22. Thomas, *New American Standard*, https://biblehub.com/ greek/4274.htm.

23. James Clear, "40 Years of Stanford Research Found That People with This One Quality Are More Likely to Succeed," *James Clear*, https://jamesclear.com/delayed-gratification.

24. *Merriam-Webster*, s.v. "intercede," www.merriam-webster.com/ dictionary/intercede.

25. Thomas, *New American Standard*, https://biblehub.com/greek/ 4697.htm.

26. *Online Etymology Dictionary*, s.v. "compassion," www.etymonline .com/word/compassion.

27. Matthew Williams, "The Prodigals Son's Father Shouldn't Have Run!," *Biola Magazine*, May 31, 2010, www.biola.edu/blogs/ biola-magazine/2010/the-prodigal-sons-father-shouldnt-have-run.

28. Helen Riess et al., "Empathy Training for Resident Physicians: A Randomized Controlled Trial of a Neuroscience-Informed

Curriculum," National Center for Biotechnology Information, May 2, 2012, www.ncbi.nlm.nih.gov/pmc/articles/ PMC3445669.

29. Stephen Trzeciak and Anthony Mazzarelli, *Compassionomics: The Revolutionary Scientific Evidence That Caring Makes a Difference* (Pensacola, FL: Studer Group, 2019).

30. Wharton Business Daily, "Can 40 Seconds of Compassion Make a Difference in Health Care?" Knowledge at Wharton, August 6, 2018, https://knowledge.wharton.upenn.edu/article/the -compassion-crisis-one-doctors-crusade-for-caring.

31. Fady Noun, "Mother Teresa, the War in Lebanon and the Rescue of 100 Orphans and Children with Disabilities," *PIME Asia News*, September 2, 2016, www.asianews.it/news-en/Mother-Teresa, -the-war-in-Lebanon-and-the-rescue-of-100-orphans-and -children-with-disabilities-38470.html.

32. Amy Summerville and Neal J. Roese, "Dare to Compare: Fact-Based Versus Simulation-Based Comparison in Daily Life," National Center for Biotechnology Information, May 1, 2009, www .ncbi.nlm.nih.gov/pmc/articles/PMC2597832.

33. Chris Heath, "18 Tigers, 17 Lions, 8 Bears, 3 Cougars, 2 Wolves, 1 Baboon, 1 Macaque, and 1 Man Dead in Ohio," *GQ*, February 6, 2012, www.gq.com/story/terry-thompson-ohio-zoo-massacre -chris-heath-gq-february-2012.

34. Lewis Howes, "Erik Weihenmayer: Success Without Seeing: Climbed Everest and Kayaked the Grand Canyon Blind," May 22, 2017, in *School of Greatness*, episode 487, podcast, video, 53:56, https://lewishowes.com/podcast/i-erik-weihenmayer.

35. Thomas, *New American Standard*, https://biblehub.com/greek/ 4735.htm.

36. Oscar Broneer, "The Apostle Paul and the Isthmian Games," *Biblical Archaeologist*, vol. 25, no. 1 (1962): 2–31, https://doi.org/ 10.2307/3211017.

37. Rick Warren, *The Purpose Driven Life: What on Earth Am I Here For?* (Grand Rapids, MI: Zondervan, 2012), 149.

38. Derek Gatopoulos, "Distance Runners Track Ancient Legend in Punishing Race," World Athletics, September 23, 1999, www .worldathletics.org/news/news/distance-runners-track-ancient -legend-in-puni.

39. Dean Karnazes, quoted in Sarah Keating, "The Secrets of Endurance Athletes," *BBC Future*, November 6, 2018, www.bbc.com/ future/article/20181106-the-secrets-of-endurance-athletes.

40. Barna defined churchgoers as those who have attended church within the past six months. See "51% of Churchgoers Don't Know

of the Great Commission," Barna, March 27, 2018, www.barna
.com/research/half-churchgoers-not-heard-great-commission.

41. "Coca-Cola History," Coca-Cola Company, www.coca
    -colacompany.com/company/history.

42. Thomas, *New American Standard*, https://biblehub.com/greek/
    2293.htm.

43. "Billy Graham Resources," Wheaton College, www.wheaton.edu/
    about-wheaton/museum-and-collections/buswell-library
    -archives-and-special-collections/research/billy-graham
    -resources; Laura Bailey, "The Night Billy Graham Was Born
    Again," Billy Graham Evangelistic Association, November 6,
    2017, https://billygraham.org/story/the-night-billy-graham-was
    -born-again.

44. Stacey King, quoted in "Among Jordan's Great Games, This Was
    It," *Los Angeles Times*, March 29, 1990, www.latimes.com/archives/
    la-xpm-1990-03-29-sp-582-story.html.

45. David E. Garland, *The New American Commentary: 2 Corinthians*,
    vol. 29 (Nashville: Broadman, Holman, 1999), 60, with quotes
    from N. Watson, *The Second Epistle to the Corinthians*, Epworth
    Commentaries (London: Epworth, 1993), 3.

46. "Are You a Christian?," Grace Evangelical Society, January 1, 2016,
    https://faithalone.org/grace-in-focus-articles/are-you-a-christian.

47. *NIV Cultural Backgrounds Study Bible: Bringing to Life the Ancient
    World of Scripture* (Grand Rapids, MI: Zondervan, 2016), 2078.

48. *Dictionary.com*, s.v. "happy," www.dictionary.com/browse/happy.

49. Kyoungmi Kim, "Happy People Does Not Compare: Difference in
    Social Comparison Between Happy and Unhappy People," *Asia-
    pacific Journal of Convergent Research Interchange*, vol. 5, no. 3 (Sep-
    tember 30, 2019), http://fucos.or.kr/journal/APJCRI/Articles/
    v5n3/3.pdf.

50. Thomas, *New American Standard*, https://biblehub.com/greek/703.htm.

51. Thomas, *New American Standard*, https://biblehub.com/greek/
    1342.htm.

52. Thomas, *New American Standard*, https://biblehub.com/greek/
    2126.htm.

53. Valerie Ross, "Numbers: The Nervous System, from 268-MPH
    Signals to Trillions of Synapses," *Discover Magazine*, May 14, 2011,
    www.discovermagazine.com/health/numbers-the-nervous
    -system-from-268-mph-signals-to-trillions-of-synapses.

54. Eric Lindberg, "Practicing Gratitude Can Have Profound Health
    Benefits, USC Experts Say," *USC News*, November 25, 2019,
    https://news.usc.edu/163123/gratitude-health-research
    -thanksgiving-usc-experts.

TIM TEBOW is a two-time national champion, Heisman Trophy winner, first-round NFL draft pick, and former professional baseball player. Tebow currently serves as a speaker, is a college football analyst with ESPN and the SEC Network, and is the author of five *New York Times* bestsellers, including *Shaken, Mission Possible, This Is the Day,* and the children's book *Bronco and Friends: A Party to Remember.* He is the founder and leader of the Tim Tebow Foundation (TTF), whose mission is to bring faith, hope, and love to those needing a brighter day in their darkest hour of need. Tim is married to Demi-Leigh Tebow (née Nel-Peters), a speaker, influencer, entrepreneur, and Miss Universe 2017. Tim and Demi live in Jacksonville, Florida, with their three dogs, Chunk, Kobe, and Paris.

www.timtebow.com
Facebook, Instagram, Twitter: @timtebow
LinkedIn: www.linkedin.com/in/timtebow15
TikTok: @timtebow_15

Check Out
Tim's Children's Books!

Also From Tim Tebow!

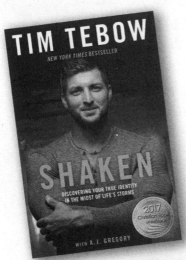

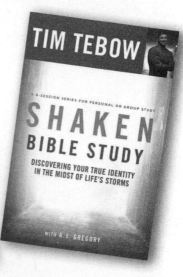

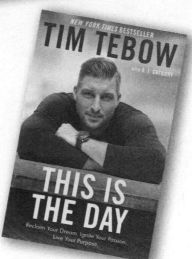